Annie O' The Mill

A Cumbrian Life Remembered

Anne Dawes

Lilma Press 2005

© Anne Dawes 2005

First published in 2005
by Lilma Press in Great Britain,
44 Belt Road, Hednesford, Cannock, Staffs, WS12 4JP.

ISBN 0 9551026 0 X

Typeset in 12½pt Monotype Perpetua
by Printdesigns Wilmslow.

CONTENTS

Acknowledgements and Dedication   2

Family Trees   4

Map   6

Chapter 1:   **A Long Walk**   7

Chapter 2:   **The Rich Man in His Castle**   20

Chapter 3:   **A Time to Live – A Time to Die**   33

Chapter 4:   **A Jar of Sweets**   46

Chapter 5:   **Yellow Pooter to Make Him Go**   58

Chapter 6:   **Scholarship and Scarlet Fever**   71

Chapter 7:   **Dancing on the Village Green**   89

Chapter 8:   **Rabbits and Rhubarb**   103

Chapter 9:   **Fire at the Mill**   114

Chapter 10:   **Taking the Goat by the Horns**   126

Chapter 11:   **Shingles in the Snow**   142

Chapter 12:   **What Kept You?**   155

For my grandchildren

ACKNOWLEDGEMENTS

This story could not have been told without the interest, encouragement and help with research of so many members of my extended family. I would like to thank Bob's daughters, Edna, Edith and Margaret; Kate's daughter, Muriel; Mary's son, Ray; John's son, Jim; George Wilkinson's granddaughter, Janet, and his son, Walton; George Irving's daughters, Mary, Dorothy and Elizabeth; my cousins, Robert and Jane, Billy's widow, Barbara; and my brother, Peter, for all their contributions and memories.

I would also like to thank Dr John Burn and Robbie Elliot of Brampton; Beamish Museum; the National Motorbike Museum; and staff of the Alma building at Carlisle Castle for help with research.

Special thanks must be given to my husband, Ed, for his support throughout the project; to my daughter-in-law, Rachael, for presentation of the family trees; and to my daughter, Janice, for help in preparing and editing the text.

Annie's Family Tree

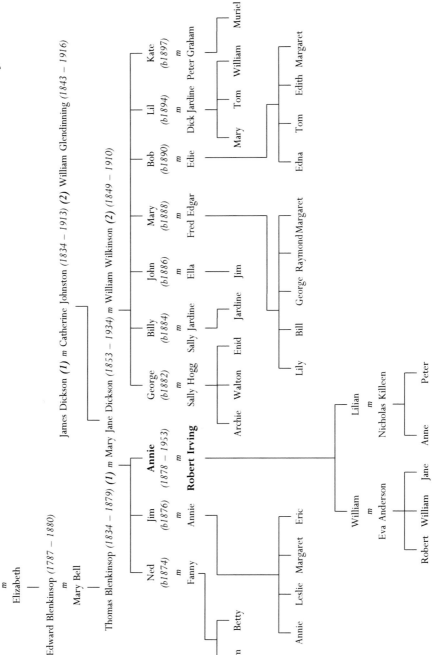

Rob's Family Tree

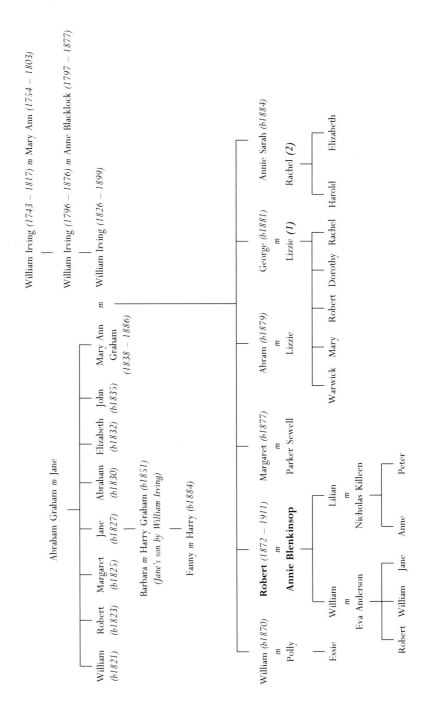

William Irving *(1743 – 1817)* *m* Mary Ann *(1754 – 1803)*

William Irving *(1796 – 1876)* *m* Anne Blacklock *(1797 – 1877)*

William Irving *(1826 – 1899)*

Abraham Graham *m* Jane

William *(b1821)*

Robert *(b1823)*

Margaret *(b1825)*

Jane *(b1827)*

Abraham *(b1830)*

Elizabeth *(b1832)*

John *(b1835)*

Mary Ann Graham *(1838 – 1886)*

m

Barbara *m* Harry Graham *(b1851)*
(Jane's son by William Irving)

Fanny *m* Harry *(b1884)*

William *(b1870)*

m

Polly

Robert *(1872 – 1911)*

m

Annie Blenkinsop

Margaret *(b1877)*

m

Parker Sewell

Abram *(b1879)*

m

Lizzie

George *(b1881)*

m

Lizzie *(1)*

Annie Sarah *(b1884)*

Rachel *(2)*

Essie

William

m

Eva Anderson

Lilian

m

Nicholas Killeen

Robert   William   Jane

Anne   Peter

Warwick   Mary

Robert   Dorothy   Rachel

Harold   Elizabeth

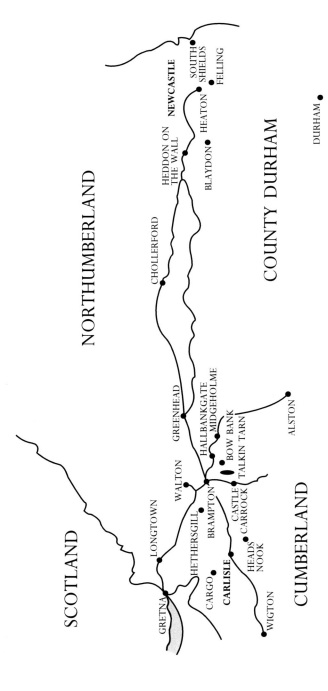

Map locating many of the towns and villages mentioned in the book. It also shows the route that Annie followed by horse and dray, in 1911, between Heaton and Walton.

1

A LONG WALK

A week after Martinmas, in November 1871, farm labourer's daughter Mary Jane Dickson left the seaside village of Gretna, in Scotland, and walked across the border into Cumberland. She was travelling twenty miles to the village of Castle Carrock, four miles beyond Brampton, in the Cumberland fells. She had walked into Brampton the previous week, for the Martinmas hirings, and returned home, delighted, with Thomas Blenkinsop's shilling. She had secured the position of housekeeper for Thomas and for his aged father, Yeoman farmer Edward Blenkinsop.

When Thomas had seen the bunch of hopefuls in Brampton Market Place he had been enchanted, first by the physical appearance of Mary Jane, and second by her soft Scottish accent. Plans for hiring a mature local woman were dismissed immediately because, as he told his father, it was a strong work-horse that was prepared to walk from Gretna to Brampton and back again in one day.

Mary Jane strode happily along. All she possessed was in the bag that swung easily from her right hand. She had a good feeling about this job. There was no mistress waiting to order her about and, at only eighteen, she would be in sole charge of the domestic scene. If she played her cards right who knew what could result?

She played her cards well. On the 2nd October, 1873, twenty-year-old Mary Jane married thirty-nine-year-old Thomas. Their first son, Edward, named after Thomas's father, was christened three months later, in January 1874. A second son, James, named after Mary Jane's father, was born two years after that, and their daughter, Ann Blenkinsop, was born on Wednesday, 10th April, 1878.

Ann's father, Thomas, died the following year when she was eighteen months old. For the next ten months her mother, Mary Jane, kept house for Ann's grandfather until he too died on 23rd July 1880, at the considerably advanced age of 93. Ann, now known as Annie, was two years old. In later years, during school playtimes, Annie often gathered posies of wild flowers and popped across the lane to lay them on the grave of her father, grandfather and grandmother. Her grandmother, Mary, was only 36 years old when, like many young women of her time, she lost her life giving birth to her youngest child, also named Mary. Annie's father, Thomas, had lost his mother when he was five years old.

In his will, proved in December 1880, her grandfather, Edward Blenkinsop, of a lineage going back to the Viking invasions, left: £50, a clock and a mahogany bedstead to his daughter Annie Currie; £50 to his daughter Mary Jane Milbourne and the residue of his personal estate (less than £50 in cash) and all his real estate to his daughter-in-law Mary Jane Blenkinsop. The real estate was in trust for his eldest grandson Edward (Ned). The rental from the properties was to be used for the maintenance, education and advancement of all three children. Mary Jane Blenkinsop was named as his executrix.

In spite of the two bereavements so soon in her life, Annie remembered a happy early childhood in Castle Carrock. The resourceful Mary Jane carried on the family business of producing and selling beer and ale, for which there was a high demand in the area, from the "brewhouse" adjoining her property. The attractive and hard working young widow soon won the admiration of William Wilkinson, a younger son of the miller of Carlatton Mill, and one of her most regular customers.

William and Mary Jane were married in 1881, and on her marriage, by the laws of the land at that time, she would have to give up all rights of property ownership to her new husband. All her furniture and household possessions, the rents from her property, all monies and jewellery, even the clothes she was wearing would now belong to him. William duly took over the running of the beer and ale house, reputedly drinking most of the profits. Mary Jane, who produced three more sons, George, Billy and John, in quick succession, often found herself in dire financial straits. On many occasions she was forced to send her older boys, Ned and Jim, accompanied by the young George, to dig up potatoes from the fields. She pushed the potatoes round the village in a wheelbarrow and sold them for money to feed and clothe her children.

In 1888, another Blenkinsop legacy enabled William and Mary Jane to acquire the tenancy of Walton Mill and farm, on the Castlesteads estate, in the beautiful Roman Wall village of Walton, some seven miles away. The previous tenants had been a family called Irving.

Annie vividly recalled her arrival in the village, riding with her five boisterous brothers on a horse drawn wagon, driven by her stepfather, and laden with all their possessions. Mary Jane, nearing the end of her seventh pregnancy, followed behind driving an equally overloaded horse and cart. Annie was ten. Her sister Mary, amid "a right carry-on", was born two days later on 30th May. Three more children, Robert, Elizabeth (Lil) and Kate were later added to the family at the Mill.

Postcard of Walton.

The Mill, powered by water, was kept working day and night. The men employed to keep it running worked shifts and slept in the building. The family lived in the nearby farmhouse. Income from the Corn Mill was supplemented by that from the Saw Mill which was also part of the property.

The affable miller was well liked in the local community. He was apparently a gregarious character whose generosity to fellow drinkers knew no bounds on his way home from market in Carlisle. His horse stopped automatically at every pub on the route and then, undriven, brought him home, lying totally inebriated, and penniless, in the back of the cart.

One April Fool's Day Annie exacted sweet revenge on her stepfather as he lay in bed sleeping off the previous day's excesses. She ran into his bedroom at 8.00 am shouting, "Quick, quick, get up! They're delivering the corn to the Granary."

When the unkempt and hastily dressed miller arrived, lurching and reeling, to find no delivery in process, a little figure behind the hedge yelled "April Gowk". She had to hide for the rest of the day but she delighted in her memories of the scene for the rest of her life.

When, as an adult, she met one of the miller's acquaintances who was eager to sing his praises as a "Great Fellow", she tartly told him about the wife and children waiting at home for his return from market. The money so generously squandered on his homeward journeys had been sorely needed for food, clothes and shoes. Significantly, every one of Mary Jane's ten children were strict teetotallers for life. Many of them, including Annie, joined the Methodist Church and signed the "pledge" at an early age.

Annie became her mother's helper from childhood. She loved, nurtured and helped to raise the four half-brothers and three half-sisters of the second marriage. She was known in the village as "Annie o' the Mill" and was often to be seen struggling between the village and the Mill with a sack of grain or flour on her shoulders, much to the distress of many of the villagers. The rounding of her shoulders in later life was the result of this childhood labour.

Work at home was never ending. Mary Jane kept a spotless house and kitchen. The stone "flags" of the kitchen floor were scrubbed daily with fine sand. The kitchen table was kept white by the same treatment. Wash day was a special trauma, especially in winter, with all the boiling, possing, mangling, drying, starching and ironing. The ironing was done with flat irons heated in the fire.

The younger children had to be watched continually. When four-year-old Billy put a bucket over his head and began racing and shouting around the deep pond in the yard, Annie was just in time to rescue him from drowning as he ran straight into the water.

Annie went to the village schools, in Castle Carrock and Walton, where she was a bright and eager scholar, avidly soaking up knowledge. "The boy stood on the burning deck," and "Into the valley of death rode the six hundred," were only two of the poems felt suitable for the children to learn by heart. Apart from the daily scripture lessons and the three Rs, knitting and sewing formed the main part of the curriculum. Annie's sampler now hangs in the home of three of her great great grandchildren at Worcester. She learned to knit socks and stockings on four needles, to darn beautifully, and to sew on patches. She also learned the correct way to sew on buttons. She often told her grandchildren of how, as a young scholar in Castle Carrock, she had been asked to bring some calico for a sewing lesson. Mary Jane produced a piece of old sheeting and then chased the young Annie all the way to school with the child bringing out the village with her screams of, "I want new calico! I want new calico!"

The sympathetic teacher quietly ushered the screaming child into school to sew her piece of old sheeting. Her needlework skills were put to good use in the winter evenings at home. No clothes were ever thrown away. When no longer fit for wear, the buttons were first removed from the garments and stored in a large button box for re-use when needed. The remaining material was sorted and cut up for a variety of uses. Some went into home-made mats. The rest became dusters, dish cloths or floor cloths according to their texture.

In winter time Mary Jane would put stones in the dying embers of the fire each night. As the children left for school in the morning they were each given a hot stone to toss between their hands on the way. Gloves were luxuries they couldn't afford. Annie remembered going to Sunday School and always laughed about the Sunday School parties. Although she often felt hungry at home – there never seemed to be enough food for so many mouths – Mary Jane always found plenty of bread and butter to fill their stomachs before they were allowed to go to the parties. Their last instructions were always, "Now don't go eating all in front of you. Don't you dare let them think you don't get fed at home!"

Poor Mary Jane was always struggling against insurmountable odds to "Keep up appearances". Respectability must be maintained at all costs. Apart from everyday clothes and Sunday Best, all the family had to have "mourning clothes" to wear if any relative died. Annie remembered the deaths of numerous unknown aunts and uncles as trials to be borne because of the year's mourning required, when only black clothes could be worn by even the youngest children. She especially remembered having a new Easter bonnet when she was six and had just come out of mourning. Unfortunately, a disobliging uncle died just before Easter Sunday and out came the old black hat. Annie thought she had the solution. Mary Jane was whitewashing a ceiling. Annie put on the black hat and stood underneath getting the hat spectacularly spattered. But Mary Jane managed to wash off all the white spots and Annie's Easter bonnet was not worn that year!

Death was an ever-present reality for Victorian children. Mary Jane was fortunate, and probably unique, in that she never suffered the loss of a beloved child. Preparations for such a catastrophe, however, were always in place and her children regularly lost familiar faces from their classroom. "Laying Out" clothes, for themselves and their children, were part of every "respectable" family's possessions. These included the best possible quality nightdress for the women, or nightshirt for the men, and a suitable matching nightcap. White linen sheets and pillow cases were also kept ready for such events when unavailabilty of suitable items would be considered the ultimate disgrace.

When friends, neighbours or relatives died, they would be lain out in a bedroom or front parlour, and Mary Jane would take her children to pay their respects. Annie became used to viewing the dead, and with the natural curiosity and interest of childhood, took a clinical view of many of the bodies she saw displayed. She witnessed first hand the horrors of corpses that had not been properly attended immediately after death. Staring eyes, sagging jaws and gaping mouths were, she noted, to be avoided at all costs.

While still in her teens, she was often called upon to help her mother with the laying-out of villagers. She soon learned about placing pennies on the quickly closed eyelids. Tying up the jaw with a clean white handkerchief was another task that had to take place before Rigor Mortis set in. But the first priority was to stuff the back passage with cotton wool to prevent the escape of bodily waste.

An attractively laid out body gave a peaceful and comforting appearance that often eased the grieving process and helped the bereaved families through their darkest hours. For much of her adult life, when she returned to Walton with her two young children, Annie was called upon to perform this service for her neighbours. Although very often exhausted from her own lot in life, she went willingly, at any time of the day or night, to do what she could for those who needed her skills.

She would be summoned as soon as death was imminent and witnessed so many passings that she never doubted the existence of an after-life. She had a good understanding with the local doctor. On one occasion, when he was too slow to answer her summons, the old lady was already dead when he arrived. The doctor took in the scene, looked hard at Annie, felt the lady's pulse, and said quietly, "She's just gone now," thereby saving the family the distress of a post mortem and inquest.

When she was thirteen, a terrified Annie was convinced that she herself was going to die. A kindly villager, Bel Ridley, found her crying behind a wall after delivering a sack of flour. Mrs Ridley took her into her own home and despatched her husband, Matt, on a "walk around the village." She made Annie a hot drink and gently told her the facts of life. She explained that the bleeding, which would come every month, was part of every woman's life. She told her how to look after herself at these times and assured her of an open door, at any time, if any other worries beset her.

Annie vowed that no child of hers would ever suffer such torment through ignorance and false modesty. Menstruation, and where babies came from, would never be a secret in her home.

Her brother Robert (Bob) was the latest baby to have arrived at the Mill. Mary Jane now had six sons and she ruled them absolutely. The miller had an easy going personality but his wife was made of sterner stuff. When Mary told her that the toddler Bob was paddling in Cambeck she raced down to the river with Annie on her heels. She grabbed the child by his ankles and ducked him, upside down, several times in the deepest part of the water. She then threw him at Annie with the words, "Now go and get him changed." Bob never again played in the river.

It was George, a few years earlier, who had come near to drowning in Cambeck. Some of the Mill fields lay on the other side of the river and had to be accessed by large stepping stones. One day, in winter, nine-year-old George was accompanying Ned and Jim as they went, with Gelt, their border collie, to check the sheep on the other side of the swollen river. George, never one to tread carefully, hadn't noticed the ice on the stepping stones. As he skipped across after his older brothers he suddenly slipped headlong into the treacherous, freezing water. Before his brothers had moved, Gelt was in the water. The faithful dog grabbed the young boy by his collar and held him afloat until Ned and Jim could fish him out.

Her family were sure that Mary Jane herself intended a watery grave for John when she caught him stamping in a puddle, wearing his brand new, hard-worked-for boots. She ducked him so ferociously and repeatedly in the Mill pond that his brothers and sisters feared for his life. Clothes and food, she told them, did not come easily.

Although, by today's standards, food was never plentiful at the Mill during Annie's childhood, there was no starvation. There was always a basic supply of milk, butter and cheese that many town children of the time would never enjoy. But the family knew that whatever was used at home could not be sold to bring in much needed cash. Farm produce was taken every week to the small, historic market town of Brampton, three miles away.

The boys learned to trap and skin rabbits and hares, and to catch pheasants and other game birds. They could catch fish as well, if allowed away from the farm for long enough. The rivers Irthing and King ran nearby and Cambeck flowed by their door. Annie hated the job of frying eels. She maintained that they seemed to live "for ever" and wriggled so furiously in the pan that she often feared she was frying them alive.

The necks of hens no longer laying were quickly wrung to provide a Sunday dinner, although one skinny chicken had to be thinly sliced to serve so many! Annie became an expert plucker and drawer of fowl and in emergency could wring a hen's neck herself. She knew that her share of the chicken would always be the "parson's nose." No other part was ever thrown away. The giblets were cooked and made into pies. The bones were boiled for stock for huge pans of delicious broth. Feathers from the poultry, particularly duck and goose, were saved for cushions, pillows and even mattresses. The wings from the Christmas goose made grate-cleaning brushes that lasted until Christmas came again. What would Mary Jane make of today's extravagant, throw-away society?

During the laying season, eggs from the hens were pickled to see them through the leaner times.

Once a year, a pig was killed – horrifically, by today's standards. Two men, known as "pig-stickers," used to travel round the farms to kill the pigs. They were always covered in blood and the stench from their clothing alerted the pig as to their intent. One of the men had to fell the pig with a "felling hammer" while the other pushed a sharp, pointed stick into the animal's brain, twisting the stick as he did so. If they were not successful at their first attempt the pig would run squealing round the yard ("squealing like a stuck pig") while Annie's brothers chased it with sticks and helped the "pig stickers" to finish their gruesome task.

While Annie and her mother were dealing with the salting of the meat, hams and bacon, and the making of sausage and black pudding, the boys would be playing football in the farm yard with the blown up pig's bladder. The pig's trotters were made into potted meat (brawn).

There was always flour for the many loaves that had to be baked each day. Young men and boys labouring on a farm and mill had tremendous appetites. Annie, and in their turn, Mary, Lil and Kate, learned all their home cooking skills from the able Mary Jane – none of whose recipes were written down! Gingerbread, scones and rock buns were part of the stock in trade of the farm kitchen. Huge suet puddings were boiled daily. Suet dumplings or Yorkshire pudding, baked on a large tray, always accompanied the main meal to cut down on the amount of meat consumed. Fruit pies, on large plates, were baked all year round and known in Cumberland as "plate cakes." Apples were stored in trays. Plums, pears, gooseberries, cherries and rhubarb were bottled.

As the fruits ripened, jams and jellies were made in sufficient quantities to last for the year, and used sparingly to make sure they were never without. All the children were involved from their earliest years in the gathering of brambles (never called blackberries), bilberries, hazel nuts, chestnuts and crab apples. Blackcurrants, raspberries, gooseberries and rhubarb were grown at home as were all the root vegetables, cabbages, sprouts, peas and beans.

In September the mushrooms flourished and it was important to rise early, like the bird who caught the worm, to harvest them quickly from the surrounding fields. As dawn was breaking, a little army from the Mill would be emerging to fill their baskets before early breakfast and school. They never ceased to wonder at how a fresh crop, like manna from heaven, sprang up each night. The mushrooms were made into soup or fried with a small slice of bacon. The delights of such flavours can never be recaptured today.

The corn and hay were harvested in late summer and this was the Mill's busiest time. Every member of the family took to the fields to harvest by hand and "bring in the sheaves." Harvest Festivals had a meaning for the residents of Walton Mill that could never be comprehended by today's supermarket generations.

"We plough the fields and scatter," "Come ye thankful people come," and "All is safely gathered in" were sung from the heart at the Harvest Festival services.

2

THE RICH MAN IN HIS CASTLE

Seed time and harvest may have been the most significant times of the farm year, but for the children, every season brought joys and highlights to ease the hardships of life's struggle.

With winter came the freezing of the ponds and streams for sliding and skating. Wonderful slides were made on the way to school. The snow brought snowmen, and more especially, snowball fights between teams protected by speedily built snow walls and barriers. Before the snow had vanished the first snowdrops were emerging on the village green – still delighting the people of Walton into this the twenty-first century. As the year progressed, primroses, marsh marigolds, bluebells, cowslips, violets, foxgloves, buttercups and daisies all flourished in their own, sometimes secret, habitat. Wild roses adorned the hedges on the long lane up to Walton, and along the way to Walton Mill.

The mill pond was a reliable indication of the weather in store for them. They watched the water hens building their nests and knew by the height of the nests on the sides of the pond if a wet summer was ahead. Many years later Bob's daughter, Edna, won a County Prize for her observations of the water hens in the mill pond.

Shrove Tuesday, in February, saw the making and eating of giant pancakes. By now the first lambs were often gambolling in the fields. At Easter came the pasche eggs. Eggs were individually wrapped in onion peel saved over the year. An outer wrapping of newspaper or cloth tied with string kept the peel in place. Sometimes, primrose heads and delicately shaped leaves or ferns were placed inside the onion peel. The eggs were simmered in boiling water for up to two hours. Every egg that was unwrapped had a different, beautiful pattern to be admired. Disorganised or over-worked housewives simply boiled their eggs in water containing loose onion peel – but these were dyed plain brown all over. Children often acquired large collections of pasche eggs given to them by neighbours, friends and relatives. If they were lucky an orange was given as well. A bowl of pasche eggs formed the centre piece of the tea table on Easter Sunday.

May Day saw great celebrations on the village green. As a child, Annie danced around the May Pole before joining in the sports and games that followed. She particularly enjoyed watching the village youths vying for superiority on the greasy pole. Two youths faced each other astride the pole and each held a pillow to attack the other and try to gain victory by unseating him.

Fine summer weekends were the best for visiting relatives at Castle Carrock. The journey was sometimes made on foot, and sometimes by horse and cart. The quieter Annie remained during these visits the more interesting became the snippets of conversation, often spoiled by a sudden, "little jugs have big ears," from an ever vigilant Mary Jane.

By the 12th August the Squire and his friends were in residence at Castlesteads for the shooting. When the shooting party was in the Walton Mill area Mary Jane was required to feed the entire party of shooters and beaters at the Mill farm, with provisions supplied by the Squire. This meant more work than usual for Mary Jane and Annie. Mary Jane's cleaning reached fever pitch before the Upper Classes descended upon her and the entire family were strictly schooled in expected standards of behaviour. The Mill had two adjoining "kitchens" and Upstairs/Downstairs prevailed in the organisation of the catering. The gentry were seated in the "top" kitchen and the beaters were kept in their place in the "lower" kitchen. The children watched, wide eyed, as vast quantities of food were consumed, desperately waiting for the left-overs to come their way.

In autumn, school playtimes were devoted to conkers, strung on boot or shoe laces. Any laces snapped during the year were saved for this purpose.

Halloween was celebrated in and around the barn with turnip lanterns – the dug out turnip was used in broths and stews. Apples were hung on strings from the barn rafters and had to be bitten with hands kept behind the back. There was also ducking for apples in a tin bath of water. A sharp and wary eye was kept for any restless spirits that might be at large in the area. The next day, All Saints Day, meant a visit to church. The village school was Church maintained and the Church calendar was strictly followed. The vicar visited the school every week to test the children on their catechism. Annie was confirmed when she was twelve.

Huge bonfires were built to celebrate Guy Fawkes Night and potatoes were placed in the hot ashes that remained, to cook slowly overnight. They made a warm and delicious, if somewhat unusual, breakfast the next morning.

Preparations for Christmas soon followed. Plum puddings, boiled in cloths, and rich fruit cakes were made early so that they had time to mature and reach their best for Christmas Day. Nearer the time, vast quantities of mince pies, filled with home made mince meat, were baked. Geese, ducks and cockerels had to be killed and prepared for sale locally. Plenty of feathers were thus made available for use next year! Their own goose had to be stuffed with a home made stuffing of sage, onions and breadcrumbs.

The farmhouse was decorated with holly and mistletoe gathered locally. Eyes had been kept peeled during the previous weeks for the holly trees bearing the best red berries. Presents were few, but each stocking usually contained one small offering for each eager recipient together with a piece of fruit and, if times were not too hard, a silver threepenny bit. Family Christmases at the Mill were among Annie's happiest childhood memories. She remembered chestnuts spitting and dancing as they roasted by the fire and the coming together of the whole village for Carol Services in the Church. "Once in Royal David's City" was her own special favourite.

New Year followed in quick succession. Being so close to the Scottish border, and Mary Jane being of Scottish descent, the New Year customs of the Scots were also observed. First Footing was taken very seriously and a suitable candidate, bearing a nugget of coal, was carefully lined up, well in advance, to ensure that only good fortune would befall them in the year ahead.

So the seasons came and went as each new life arrived to swell the family numbers. The youngest member of the family was Kate, born on 27th March 1897, when Mary Jane was 44 years old. All through her adult life, Annie marvelled at the ease with which her mother had always seemed to give birth. She witnessed her scrubbing down the stairs at 10pm, less than two hours before the arrival of her youngest child. Within days she was up and about and ruling the roost once more. At Kate's birth, nineteen-year-old Annie was Mary Jane's main helper. She had also been in attendance when Lil arrived three years earlier. Mary Jane – by now well established as an unofficial village mid-wife – remained in charge throughout her own confinements.

Annie's clearest memories of Lil's birth were of the Christening which came soon afterwards. Having slaved throughout the day with preparations for the event, Annie was suddenly required to knit a pair of socks for three-year-old Bob, so that he wouldn't shame them next day at the baby's Christening. She kept falling asleep over the task and was constantly poked and slapped by her mother to "wake up and get on with the job." In the end Mary Jane finished the socks herself and everyone was respectable when the relatives arrived.

No doubt the cleanliness of Mary Jane's home, the fresh country air, and the basic farm food would all help to preserve the health and relatively strong constitutions of her family. They all managed to survive the childhood illnesses that afflicted them. Annie played an active part in nursing the younger members of the family, as her mother had nursed her, through whooping cough, measles, mumps and chicken pox, as well as all the coughs and colds that beset them.

Wheezy chests were rubbed with goose fat and covered with flannel. Soothing drinks of blackcurrant tea, made by adding boiling water to a spoonful of blackcurrant jam, were offered to young invalids, along with concoctions of honey and lemon. Small quantities of butter and sugar mashed together in a saucer were eased down infected throats. Stuffed up noses and bronchial passages were cleared by the sufferer sitting at a table with a towel covering both his head and a bowl of steaming Friars Balsam diluted with boiling water.

Little bodies, aflame with high temperatures, were bathed frequently and the patients kept comfortable in clean, warm beds. Annie spent many nights watching by sick beds as fevers raged and young children struggled to breathe. Cooling jugs of fresh water were always at hand for drinks that would prevent dehydration.

Most of the Mill children managed to fall, at some point in their young lives, into the beds of stinging nettles that grew so lavishly in the area. Annie was constantly pulling dock leaves, always found close by, to apply to the resulting angry rashes.

A small cotton bag was filled with salt and warmed in the oven for sufferers of terrible toothache. They could lie the affected cheek on the bag and obtain some relief from their torment.

Annie always regarded her sister Mary, ten years her junior, as her "special" charge. Mary was the delicate one of the brood and suffered more than the rest from a steady stream of infections. In 1902, when Mary was fourteen, and Annie was no longer living at home, the doctor advised that removal of her tonsils would be the best way to put an end to her constant illnesses. Mary Jane was instructed to scour the already spotless white table and daughter Mary was told to lie on it and open her mouth. Without further ado, and with his instruments in full view of the victim, the doctor snipped out her tonsils and her mother mopped up the blood. The patient was sat in a comfortable chair to recover from her ordeal.

"My mother was a very hard woman," Mary later recalled, "but my father was always very kind to me."

Mary's health did not save her from the hard physical labour that Mary Jane demanded of all her children. She was not allowed to stay on at school and train as a teacher, as she so desperately wanted. Instead, her mother put her to work with her brothers in the fields. In later life, she often commented sadly on the size of her hands, which she felt had been greatly enlarged by the manual labour endured in her youth.

Walton, on the Roman Wall, is one of the many small villages and hamlets that sprang up around the ancient market town of Brampton. Historians believe that Walton was there long before the Romans came and, like other villages and towns of that name, was called after the Celts who travelled from Wales to settle in the area. Being so close to the Scottish and Northumberland borders, the area's history has been long and turbulent, with many violent episodes.

In 1746, while Annie's ancestors were farming in Castle Carrock, six Scotsmen were dragged through the streets of Brampton on a hurdle before being hung, drawn and quartered for their support of Bonnie Prince Charlie. Information of the imminence of this event quickly spread around the area. Seventeen-year-old Thomas Blenkinsop, great-uncle of Annie's grandfather Edward, was one of a group of young men from Castle Carrock who walked into Brampton to witness the ghastly executions. By this terrible action, the good people of Brampton demonstrated their absolute loyalty to the rightful king. They saved the little border town and its surrounding villages from the dreadful retribution of George's pursuing armies, who showed no mercy to any community that gave succour to either Charles Edward Stuart or any of his followers.

By the end of the nineteenth century, however, the area was much more peaceful. Public events in Brampton were more joyful occasions relating to Queen Victoria's Diamond Jubilee, the welcoming in of the twentieth century, and the coronation of Edward the seventh. The economy of the villages surrounding Brampton depended mainly on farming and its supporting industries. Every small community had its own blacksmith, joiner, village shop and public house. The Black Bull at Walton has now capitalised on the Roman Wall connection and become The Centurion.

Employment prospects for young people wanting to stay in their home area were very limited. Apart from a Tweed Mill and Tannery in Brampton and small drift coal mines on Tindal Fell, there was little on offer. As they grew up, the family at Walton Mill became increasingly frustrated by the lack of opportunity to better themselves, aggravated, in their case, by the drunkenness and wastefulness of the head of the family. He couldn't be trusted to take a cow to market and bring home the proceeds of the sale. There was no money to pay even minimal wages to the young people slaving so hard to fund his extravagant ways. Each, in their turn, began to look further afield, often spurred on by a desire to marry and set up their own homes with their chosen sweethearts.

Annie's choice, her first and only love, was Robert Irving, a talented young carpenter who had first seen his future wife when, as a sixteen-year-old apprentice in the village he had stepped outside the workshop to watch the arrival of the new residents of Walton Mill. He had spotted, with some amusement, the young girl frantically trying to prevent her two-year-old brother falling off the wagon on which they were all so unceremoniously piled.

"This lot'll liven up the place a bit," he later remembered thinking.

Livening up the place was not an unknown pastime for Robert Irving. He was famed in the village for two incidents in particular during his short time at the village school. The school was built on the village green, in the centre of the village, and the children played on the green at school playtimes. The school lavatories, dry closets with opening doors at the back to allow for the changing of buckets, were set apart from the school. One day the enterprising young Robert gathered himself a bunch of nettles, and as each girl sat on the lavatory, he thrust the nettles up through the door at the back with wonderful effect! He was, of course, soundly thrashed for his efforts.

Another time, when he felt that nothing of very much interest was happening in village life, he didn't walk dutifully into school with the rest of the children when the bell was rung. Instead, he gathered up a goose from the many that roamed at will on the green, and with the goose under his arm he climbed up onto the school roof. The children had just taken their places when they were suddenly joined, via the chimney, by a flapping and honking, soot-covered goose!

Rob's ancestors had themselves once held the tenancy of Walton Mill, and he remembered playing in the Mill kitchen as a young boy visiting his grandparents. He was the second child of the four sons and two daughters of farm labourer William Irving and his wife Mary Ann. They were not young parents. In 1851, as a young man of twenty-five, William Irving had emigrated to Australia with his friend Abraham Graham, unaware of the fact that Abraham's sister, Jane, was expecting his child. William and Jane's son, Harry Graham, was born towards the end of the year and Jane's life in the village was not easy.

When the news of her predicament reached the absent father he had to save up for his passage money before he could return, and by then Jane no longer wanted him. In1867, sixteen years after Harry's birth – and the year that all working men got the vote, William married Jane's younger sister, Mary Ann, with Jane as one of the witnesses to the marriage.

There were already too many mouths to feed at Walton Mill, so William got himself a job as a farm labourer. He and Mary Ann went to Middlesceugh, near Carlisle, where four of their six children were born. They returned to their home village in 1880 and had two more children before Mary Ann's death in 1886. Rob was then fourteen and his youngest sister, Annie Sarah, was only two years old. Abram was seven and George was five. The eldest brother, William, was already hired on a farm outside the village. Harry Graham was, by now, married himself and had a son, another Harry who, at two years old, was the same age as his father's youngest child, Annie Sarah.

Rob's mother, Mary Ann, and his sister, Maggie.

Rob's sister, Margaret Jane (Maggie), had to take over the running of the family home when her mother died. She was only nine years old and her childhood ended at that moment. Rob, her father and other families in the village, helped as much as they could, but it was Maggie who bore the greatest burden. None of the children ever forgot the unkindness with which they were treated by Aunt Jane, their mother's sister, but Harry Graham's wife, Barbara, more than made up for this. She became "like a second mother" to her husband's younger half-brothers and sisters.

"Hill Bottom," their house in Walton (long since demolished), was an original wattle and daub cottage, one of the many "clay dabbings" built on and around the village green. In winter time, until Rob had acquired the skills to do something about it, the snow used to blow through the badly fitting window frame and into the bedroom where the brothers slept.

The Irving family, and the new family at Walton Mill, were often to be seen in each other's company, and, as the years passed, Annie and Rob found that they had much in common. Rob's outrageous sense of humour was only one of the aspects of his character that attracted Annie. Like her, he had an honest and forthright personality and a strong social conscience. From an event soon after her arrival in Walton, Rob knew that Annie had a spirit and determination to match his own. She had happened to be in the village one day as the Squire passed through, and she saw, with amazement, that all the women and girls curtsied subserviently as he went by, and the men and boys doffed their caps. The all-powerful Squire, immediately noticing the girl who hadn't given the obligatory curtsey, asked angrily, "Who are you?"

"I'm Annie," she said, looking him straight in the face, "Annie o' the Mill."

Later that afternoon, a pony and trap, driven by one of the Squire's servants, drew up at the Mill. The servant instructed Mary Jane and the Miller, "You're both to come with me. The Squire wants to see you."

They were duly transported to Castlesteads and ushered into the drawing room where the Squire was waiting for them.

"You have a daughter who doesn't know her position in life," he told them, "if she doesn't learn to show me proper respect I'll have you out of the Mill."

When the deflated couple returned to their anxious, waiting family at the Mill with their humiliating tale, their young sons were furious at their treatment, and a defiant Annie insisted,

"He's not the Queen. I'm not curtseying to him." She kept a low profile whenever she saw him approaching, but she never curtsied to the Squire. Not once.

Annie and Rob were both members of the tiny, primitive Methodist Chapel in the village, built in 1858, and regularly attended by some of Mary Jane's descendants, until its closure in 2003. Their deep and practical Christian faith was central to their lives. Annie's older brothers, Ned and Jim, also devout Methodists, both became local preachers in the Brampton circuit and walked, whatever the weather, to conduct the services in all the outlying chapels. Their friends, Rob and Abram (Abe), two of the four Irving brothers, often went along to keep them company.

Annie, who had a beautiful singing voice, went with them to lead the congregational singing. Many of the chapels had neither organs nor organists at this time. The cheerful band of young people encouraged each other along the often difficult treks to and from the chapels with

Walton Methodist Chapel.

friendly banter, philosophical discussions and laughing referral to their own "Pilgrim's Progress."

Like the Blenkinsops and Wilkinsons, the Irvings were all strict teetotallers. The Countess of Carlisle, Lady Rosalind, was active in the campaigns of the time to get young people to sign the pledge and thereby avoid lives of poverty and degradation caused by drink. Mary Jane's children needed little persuasion. The older Wilkinson boys felt, if anything, even more bitter than their Blenkinsop half-siblings about their father's drinking habits.

George, who was regularly despatched to the Black Bull for jugs of ale, reduced the rest of them to tears of horrified laughter one evening when he told them that he had "pissed" in the jug that he had just handed to the miller. One night, when his sons had reached young manhood, and William rolled home from a long convivial evening with his cronies in the Black Bull, an incandescent George, helped by brother Billy, threw him into the mill pond. As the miller emerged from the water he bewailed the fact that it was his "own sons" – not Ned and Jim, his step-sons – who had treated him so shamefully.

The brothers were so sickened by the evils of drink that they were determined to protect their younger sisters from any involvement with young men who were not strictly teetotal. When they discovered that Mary had a tryst with a young man who was known to partake of the forbidden ale, George, Billy and John dressed themselves up in their best clothes and marched along with her to the meeting. The boyfriend got the message and poor Mary chose more carefully next time!

3

A TIME TO LIVE – A TIME TO DIE

Rob saved long and hard for the delicate ruby engagement ring that he gave to Annie on her 21st birthday, the 10th April 1899. They knew that it would be a long engagement if they were to have a good start to their life together, and Rob had responsibilities at home. As the son whose employment was based in the village, he was the one who became the breadwinner for his elderly father, and for his sister, Maggie, who kept house for them. Two of his brothers, William and Abe, unable to see any future for themselves as low paid farm labourers, went to live, and work for The Railway, in the North East. His youngest sister, Annie Sarah, and brother George, were employed in the Croglin area.

Rob's father, the returned émigré William Irving, died at the age of seventy-four, just before the dawn of the new century. Maggie left home to become a live-in housekeeper and Rob took the hard decision to stop trying to earn a decent living as a village carpenter and followed his two brothers to the North East. The family had to give up their cottage at Walton and Rob went into lodgings in Newcastle-on-Tyne. He got a regular wage working as a Rolleyman for a Carting Contractor in the city, but he kept all his tools.

Annie, in the meantime, had told Mary Jane that she could no longer work without pay. She had found herself a job as a parlour maid, on Brampton Road in Carlisle, with a family called Johnstone. She and Rob were now over fifty miles apart, but they wrote regularly, and Rob travelled to Carlisle every few weeks by train.

Sometimes, in summer, they both travelled to Brampton Junction and walked from there to nearby Talkin Tarn. The walk around the tarn remains a popular leisure activity to this day. Annie would bring a picnic with her and she and Rob sometimes hired a rowing boat to row across the tarn. The tarn has always been one of the most attractive sporting arenas in the country and, in August 1901, the rowing club held a regatta and fireworks display that was much enjoyed by Rob and Annie on one of their days together.

Life with the Johnstones was much easier than it had ever been at the Mill. She had regular hours, clearly defined duties and time to call her own. Mrs Johnstone noted, with approval, the rapport that Annie soon established with the children of the family, and was delighted to have found someone so capable of standing in on both the nanny's and the cook's days off. Annie helped the children with their school work and encouraged them with their piano practice, sitting with them in her own time and learning, with them, to make sense of the music.

"When we have children," she wrote to Rob, "I want them to have a good education. I want them to have books and music."

In this, as with everything, she was many years ahead of her time, in her thinking, and how she looked at life. She was given free access to the books that Mrs Johnstone herself enjoyed. She read Dickens and Thomas Hardy, the Brontes and Jane Austen, and the novels of Annie S. Swan. When Mrs Johnstone talked to her about life at the Mill, and found out about Mary Jane's struggles to raise her large family, she passed on all her own children's outgrown clothes which Annie duly transported back to Walton.

On her evenings off in Carlisle, Annie attended the Girls Friendly Society. When she said "Goodbye" to her friends in Carlisle, in September 1903, to make final preparations for her wedding, The G.F.S. presented her with a certificate proclaiming the verse from Proverbs:

"Who can find a virtuous woman?
For her price is far above rubies.
The heart of her husband doth safely trust in her.
She will do him good and not evil all the days of her life."

Rob had found a flat for them to rent in Newcastle and she went there by train to choose their furniture from the Sale Rooms and to measure up the windows for curtains. One piece of furniture that she didn't have to choose was the rocking chair that Rob had made for her, as his own wedding present to his new bride.

The wedding breakfast was to be held at the Mill and Mary Jane, Annie and Mary all worked flat out on the cleaning and catering preparations for the event. Annie covered the cost of it all from her own savings.

Annie and Rob's
wedding photograph.

Annie and Rob were married on Tuesday, 17th November, 1903, at Walton Methodist Chapel. The bride's sister, Mary, was bridesmaid and the groom's brother, Abram, was best man. Annie, who was given away by her eldest brother, Ned, had chosen a fashionable pale grey wedding dress that she would be able to wear on many occasions in the future. The wedding was followed by the family reception at Walton Mill before the bride and groom were driven by horse and cart to Brampton Junction to travel to their new home, 82 Morley Street, Heaton, Newcastle-on-Tyne. Abe travelled back with them and helped with the transporting of the chest of wedding presents and Annie's personal belongings.

The next six years were the happiest of Annie's life. Rob's carpentry skills were soon needed again to make a cradle for their son, William, born on 19th December, 1904, and named after Rob's late father.

In the spring, following Will's birth, Mary Jane set out on a great adventure. Accompanied by seven-year-old Kate and ten-year-old Lil, she took her first train ride, and went on a trip to Newcastle to visit Annie! Annie, proudly carrying Will, met them at the station and took them home by tram. They stayed overnight so that Annie could take them across the city next day to visit Mary Jane's own mother, the elderly Kate Glendinning, who had moved to Newcastle after her second marriage. They had plenty to talk about, and it was late afternoon before Annie finally saw her mother and sisters onto the train back to Brampton Junction, a ride into Brampton on Elliot's horse-bus, and then a long walk home to the Mill.

Walton Village School, circa 1905/6. In identical dresses, Lil is fourth from the left on the third row, Kate is second on the left on the second row.

Granny Glendinning's ability to talk caused some upset to Annie and Rob later in the year. Annie had baked one of her wonderful fruit cakes for the old lady's birthday and Rob promised to deliver it after he came home from work. It was dark and late by the time he had walked across the city, but the delighted old lady kept him talking for hours and then gave him two china cups and saucers for Annie as he left. He put one cup and saucer in each of his two jacket pockets and set off for home. Within a hundred yards of his own home he was stopped and searched by the police who, on finding the cups and saucers, suspected him of burglary. They walked him back to Granny Glendinning's and knocked her up to prove his innocence. He then had to walk all the way home again.

"What kept you?" asked Annie, as he staggered through the door.

Over the next few years, life continued happily for the little family. Before long, Rob's youngest brother, George, also came to live and work in the North East. He lodged with Rob and Annie while he saved for his own marriage to Lizzie Warwick, a young woman that he had met at Croglin. The friendship that was cemented now, between George Irving and his brother's family, was to last a lifetime.

Annie's own brother, George Wilkinson, became the centre of attention in Walton, in 1905, when he married Sally Hogg. George had idolised Sally for many years but she was adamant, no doubt from having witnessed life at the Mill, that she would never be a farmer's wife. She dreamed of one day owning a house like "Friarsgarth," the finest house in Walton, and filling it with beautiful furniture and ornaments.

George gave up farming to find work and a small flat in Sunderland with which to tempt her to the altar. Their marriage was to have been the wedding of the year at Walton. Everyone at the Mill had new outfits. Rob volunteered to look after Will for the day so that Annie could travel from Newcastle to join in the celebrations. Jim and his wife came from Preston. Mary Jane made sure that everybody in the village knew what a splendid occasion it was going to be and they all turned out to watch. To delight his new bride, George had secretly ordered a wagonette to transport her and her father, Archie Hogg, from their cottage in the village to the Church. It cost a lot of money. Archie was not impressed. He refused to join his daughter in the wagonette and marched along beside it, berating her for her grand ideas.

George saw his tearful bride approaching the altar, in furious argument with her father, and went to meet them to find out what was causing her distress. He immediately landed a well-aimed fist on his future father-in-law's nose. His brothers dragged him off and Archie left the Church for First Aid. The wedding went ahead with the Miller stepping into Archie's shoes to give away his future daughter-in-law to his son. The vicar, no doubt equally keen to finish the proceedings, raised no objection. The row continued outside and the large crowd of spectators, mostly women and children, got more entertainment than they had anticipated. A lot of the men of the village were later heard to express their disappointment at having missed it all. The reception was curtailed and the happy couple were quickly removed to Brampton Junction by the bridegroom's brothers. Annie caught a later train. Mary Jane said that she'd never be able to hold up her head again. Annie commented wryly, "Well you did say that the village were going to see a wedding they wouldn't forget."

A hundred years later there are still people living in Walton who sometimes recall the "carry on" they had been told about at George and Sally's wedding.

Sally did eventually make peace with her father. She gave his name to her eldest son and called the second after their home village. George and Sally's son, Walton, became an academic and got his M.A. at Durham. His older brother, Archie, joined the Merchant Navy. Sally finally got her dream house, in Felling-on-Tyne, in 1927. She named it "Friarsgarth."

Annie returned from the wedding with plenty to tell Rob, who wished he'd been able to go with her! They settled down again into their daily routine. They belonged to the local Methodist Church but their daily life was quite different to that of life in a village. Most of Annie's shopping was done from traders calling their wares in the street beneath her window. Fish, particularly, was inexpensive and plentiful and Annie learned new cooking skills, like how to pickle herrings! She had no need to skimp and save in the ways of her childhood but she couldn't bear waste of any kind. One day, when a minute sample of margarine was pushed through their letter-box she wondered if she might "be able to fry something in it."

"Oh no you won't," said Rob, and threw it on the fire.

But it was Rob himself who told his son, as they were sitting down to a meal of sausages, "Now remember, Willy, little bites of sausage and big bites of bread!"

Annie spent a lot of time teaching her bright and clever son, who could read, write and do simple sums long before he started school. On one, never-to-be-forgotten day, when she had let him out to play with his friends in the street, she looked out of her window and saw that he was missing. She ran up and down the street searching and calling his name. Eventually a man told her that he had seen a small boy walking along the path beside the railway. She ran frantically along the path and saw a small figure, deep in thought, walking back towards her.

"What were you worrying about?" he asked her. "I was just thinking. There's so much to think about."

In the Spring of 1910, Annie's joy at knowing she was pregnant again was marred by her concerns for Rob. He looked tired and worn. In spite of all the good food she prepared he was losing weight. Soon he was unable to go to work and by late summer he was hospitalised in the city Infirmary. Throughout their time together, they had carefully put money aside for a rainy day. And the rains came. During the pregnancy that should have been so joyous, Annie realised that she was going to lose her beloved Rob. The doctors diagnosed cancer of the stomach. She had to be calm and strong – for Rob, for Will and for the unborn child – but these were her darkest and poorest days.

All Mary Jane's training in stretching money and "making do" came into force. Every day, even when heavily pregnant, Annie saved the tram fare by walking from Morley Street to the hospital to visit Rob. She used only a minimum amount of the precious savings. A good friend gave Will the tea that she had left for him after school and looked after him until her return. Sometimes he was able to visit with her, and when he couldn't go to the hospital the little boy wrote letters to his father.

As Annie sat by Rob's bedside, talking during the times he was awake, she worked quietly at her knitting and sewing. She had a layette to prepare and a growing schoolboy to keep clothed and fed. There were no State benefits. Every beautiful little item of clothing that she stitched, every sheet, shawl and blanket for the new baby was "something new from something old."

In early November a letter came from the Mill to say that her stepfather had suffered a massive stroke, was unable to speak, and was not expected to recover. Mary Jane and Annie were both "widows in waiting." Annie, herself, did not eat as well as she should have done. On 20th November she gave birth to a daughter who was so tiny and frail that as the midwife put her to her mother's breast, she said quietly, "I've sent for the minister, Annie. We'll need to get her Christened."

The concerned neighbours who gathered for the ceremony simply said, "You'll never rear her, Annie."

"I'll rear her," said Annie, "I'll call her Lilian Mary. I like the name Lilian. Mary's after her two grandmothers, Mary Jane and Mary Ann."

As soon as she could, she and Will went to the hospital to show Rob his new daughter, who didn't seem to know that she wasn't supposed to survive. He smiled tears of joy through the pain, "I wish you were back in Walton," he fretted, "you need to be back with your own folk."

"When I go back," she told him firmly, "you'll come with me."

Will's next letter to his father read:

> "Dear Dada, I hope you will still be a little bit better tomorrow. The baby does not let mama get her work done but aunt Maggie came in and nurst her for a little bit. We are going to Mrs Warhursts for tea next Monday and I am going myself after school but I know the number, it is 96 chopmere street. Do you think we will enjoy ourselves? I hope we do. Love from Willie."

On the 10th December William Wilkinson died at Walton Mill and was laid to rest in Walton churchyard. His son Billy took over the running of the farm and mill for the time being, but Mary Jane was very much in charge.

Rob was becoming noticeably weaker, and together he and Annie planned what she was going to do and how she and the children would survive. Rob wrote to "Young" Harry Graham, who was now farming at Town Head Farm, opposite the chapel in Walton. "Young" Harry had built, and bought, property in the village and Rob asked him if he would be able to let Annie have a cottage to rent as soon as one became available. Harry was only too willing to do this. Annie wrote to Mary Jane to tell her of their plans and Mary Jane wrote back to say that when the time came she must first come home to the Mill.

Annie began to pack and get everything ready for the journey that awaited her. She knew that when the time did come she would have to leave quickly. In March, Mary Jane told her youngest daughter, Kate, now a pupil at the Secondary School in Brampton, that because of all the trouble they were in, she must leave school immediately on her 14th birthday, the 27th March, and travel to Newcastle to help her sister Annie. The day after Kate's arrival Annie carried the now thriving, four-month-old baby, into the ward and found Rob sleeping. He opened his eyes and said, "Let me see my little girl." Annie held up the baby and saw him smile before he fell asleep. He never woke again.

"Why did he have to die?" his son asked. Some years later Dr Irving looked up his father's medical notes and finally answered his own question.

On the 30th March 1911, the day after Rob's death, a horse and dray with a driver up front, left Morley street in Newcastle-on-Tyne and set off across Northumberland for Walton. Beside the driver sat a fourteen-year-old girl in mourning clothes. Between the girl and a young woman dressed in black, and holding a small baby, sat a sombre-faced six-year-old boy. Just behind them, draped in black, was a coffin. Behind the coffin, suitably protected against the elements, were all their worldly goods – a bedroom suite, brass bedstead and feather bed; kitchen table and chairs; clocks, oil lamps and assorted candle sticks; the best china tea-set, crockery, pots, pans and baking tins; mixing bowls and basins; bedding boxes, curtains and clothing; a precious rocking chair and cradle; groceries and other provisions; a wash tub, rubbing board, posser and mangle; and, to the amazement of the driver, several boxes of jam jars.

They avoided the city centre and went from Heaton through the districts of Jesmond and Blakelaw. As they travelled the people, on their early morning way to work, stood silently and respectfully until they passed by. At Heddon-on-the-Wall they joined the old Military Road that stretched interminably in front of them. Although spring had come again, everything still looked bleak and desolate, but for the little boy it was all fresh and new.

Annie and Kate aroused his interest by getting him to notice how closely the long straight road followed the Roman Wall. He was also amazed at the distance between each stone built habitation visible from the road. When he commented on what seemed to be a never ending trek, they talked about how it must have been for the Roman soldiers who had marched along that very road so many years ago. As they topped one hill, another loomed in front of them – on and on with the same bleak moorland on either side and the impressive remains of Hadrian's Wall to their right. It was difficult to decide which of the grey/white blobs in the fields were sheep and which were boulders.

The weather was kind to them. Every so often they stopped to see to the baby, to rest and water the horse, and to have a small picnic at the side of the road. They passed through Chollerford and on into Greenhead, where they all dismounted and walked up the long steep bank to ease the horse's burden. It was late afternoon when they turned off onto the road for Brampton and finally crossed the border into Cumberland. They came through Brampton and turned right onto the Longtown Road, over the narrow Irthing Bridge and then right again into the lane up to Walton. As his children made their first journey up that lane, Robert Irving made his last.

Now the signs of spring were everywhere. For a child there could have been no better introduction to the way to the village where they were to make their home. Lambs were in every field and the hedgerows were bursting with new life.

"What's that big house over there?" Will asked, pointing across the fields to his left.

"That's Castlesteads," said Annie, "that's where the squire lives."

As they neared the village, they saw two young men waiting. Billy and Bob, two of her younger brothers, had come to meet them and take them home to the Mill. Quietly, they walked either side of the horse and escorted them through the silent village, where all the inhabitants stood outside their houses to show, by this action, what they felt and couldn't speak.

A warm welcome awaited the travellers who, along with their driver, were ushered straight into the farm kitchen for rest and refreshment. Willing hands took over the stabling of the horse and unloading of the dray. The coffin was carried carefully to a specially prepared side-room and placed on a bed covered with a linen sheet. All their belongings were stored in a dry corner of the barn and carefully covered. A bed was prepared for the driver and he was given a hearty breakfast before his departure next morning. He told them that he did not usually receive such hospitality.

The children were made especially welcome. Kate and Lil looked after the baby and the young men took Will around the farm and introduced him to his new way of life. Annie was amused, but horrified, to find that there was one part of his upbringing she had sadly neglected. He didn't know that milk came from cows. His was always bought in a can from a man in the street. He was very reluctant to try the liquid that he had seen coming from a cow's udder!

Two days after their arrival, a freshly scrubbed farm cart, draped with black and pulled by a well-groomed horse, carried Rob's coffin, with Kate's home made wreath of spring flowers, from the home of his ancestors, to the village church. He was to be buried beside his great grandparents, another William and another Mary Ann. Billy and Bob walked either side of the horse. Annie and Will walked hand in hand behind the cart followed by all their family, the Irvings, the Grahams, the Blenkinsops and the Wilkinsons. She had kept her promise. She had brought him back to Walton.

4

A JAR OF SWEETS

That April Fool's Day in 1911, the sun shone gloriously as Annie, tightly gripping the hand of her small son, turned away from the grave-side and took the first firm steps into the rest of her life. As the anxious, trusting, face looked up at hers the awful responsibility almost overwhelmed her and the pain of her grief was a terrible knife, tearing at the knots inside her.

"Come on," she said brightly, "let's get back to the Mill and see what Kate and Lilian are up to. We'll bring Lilian down to see the flowers later, shall we?"

They stayed at the Mill until late summer when Rose Cottage, in the very heart of the village, became vacant and they could have a home of their own once more. Rose Cottage stood beside The Green Cottage, which was joined onto the imposingly named "The Grove" cottage. In later years Rose cottage was renamed Myrtle Cottage and extended to join onto The Green Cottage.

View of the village green, showing school on left and two-roomed Rose Cottage (later Myrtle Cottage) at the end of the row across the road.

The three cottages were set at a right angle to the road through the village with a view across the green to the Church. The village school, which Will was now happily attending, was just a few steps away on the other side of the road. The back of Rose Cottage joined the front garden of Rose House, built immediately behind it, and also at right angles to the road.

Rose Cottage had one small living kitchen, one bedroom and a tiny scullery. Their furniture and all their possessions were moved from the Mill by horse and cart and packed into the tiny cottage. Next day a sign appeared in the front window:

"JAM FOR SALE.
ORDERS TAKEN FOR BREAD
AND FRUIT LOAVES."

She had not been idle during her time at the Mill. Every jar that had travelled from Newcastle was now filled with jam. Bel Ridley bought the first jar. Annie knew that some of the villagers bought one jar of jam because they wanted to help her. They bought their second and third jars because the jam was so good. She asked them to let her have the empty jars back and this they did willingly, along with any others that they had lying around. She had bought an extra supply of baking tins, and now the really hard work, the best way to tackle grief, began. She baked bread all night in her small oven and kneaded the dough in the large basin from her wash-stand. She took orders for fruit cakes for the weekends and special occasions. She used square and rectangular baking tins so that she could cut some of the cakes into smaller slab cakes to suit smaller purses. Friday was the day for the laborious stirring and careful baking of the heavy-to-handle cake mixtures.

While the fruits were in season, she replenished her stocks and made jam in the afternoons and evenings. She baked bread through the night. She sold what she had made in the mornings and snatched a few hours sleep when she could. She looked after the baby and the school-boy. She cleaned, cooked, washed, ironed, knitted and sewed for them. She kept on smiling. She survived.

"If ever you're in that position," she told her granddaughter, many years later, with awesome foresight, "don't moan about what's happened to you. Everybody has their troubles and you don't know what crosses they have to bear. People like to see a smiling face. That's how you keep your friends."

All their water had to be carried in buckets from the pump at the bottom of the village. Coal had to be carried from their coal-house, way behind Rose House. The lavatory and the ash-tip were round there as well. At night the cottage was lit by candles and a small oil-lamp. Every day, after school, until Lilian was old enough, Will walked the half-mile to the Mill to collect their can of milk. When he was a little older, and stronger, it became his job before and after school to fetch the buckets of coal and water. Collecting water from the pump was no hardship in Annie's eyes. At the Mill, as in her childhood, they were still struggling with their buckets over the long, hilly and uneven path at the back of the farmhouse that led to Howe's Well. All their drinking water and water for the dairy had to be carried from this well. The water was ice cold and beautifully refreshing in summer. In winter they weren't quite so appreciative as they negotiated the treacherous path and tried not to stumble and slip just as they were within sight of home. Water for washing was drawn from the Mill pond where it was fed by the river.

Walton was "off the beaten track" as far as Water and Electricity supplies were concerned. Even now, in the twenty-first century, Gas has not reached the village. The Water Board finally connected them to the Mains in the nineteen-thirties. Annie's buckets of water then only had to be carried from a central tap about 50 yards away.

From midnight on Saturday until midnight on Sunday Annie, who strived throughout her life to live by the Ten

Commandments, rested from her labours and did no work except basic cooking of their own meals. While she cooked the Sunday dinner, Will, and later Lilian, walked the three miles into Brampton, in all weathers, to collect the week's supply of yeast from Smith's the Chemists. The children went to Sunday school in the afternoon and they all went to Chapel at night. Annie's Sunday afternoons were spent in writing all the letters that kept her in touch with old friends and her extended family.

Rob's three brothers, William, Abe and George, were now all married, working for the Railway, and settled in Blaydon-on-Tyne. Annie's older brother, Jim, had joined the Lancashire Police Force and lived with his Yorkshire-born wife (another Annie) in Preston. John, still single, had joined the Metropolitan Police in London. George and his wife, Sally, went first to Sunderland and then to Felling-on-Tyne.

Ned, her eldest and dearest brother, following the example of his heroes, The Tolpuddle Martyrs who, like him, had been farm labourers and Methodist local preachers, had emigrated to Ontario with his young family, determined to bring them up in a "Land of Opportunity." It had been a sad and terrible parting knowing that he would never again return to his roots, and never again see or speak to any of the family and friends left behind. Annie always had letters to write.

The Letters of Administration of Rob's estate, issued to Annie on the 25th April, 1911, confirmed that all she had in the world was the sum of sixty-eight pounds, seventeen shillings and sixpence, and that the stamp for the affidavit cost one pound and ten shillings. She put most of the money in her Post Office Savings Account at Brampton, but she knew that there was one major purchase to be made from it.

Together, she and Mary Jane chose headstones for their husbands' graves. They chose similar designs in white marble, with lettering in lead. Each stone, erected in 1912, cost £12. The two graves were situated either side of the path through the Churchyard to the Church. The miller's was just inside the gate on the left, and Rob's a few steps further up on the right.

Lilian aged 18 months.

In the autumn of 1911, Annie and Lilian, now taking her first steps, walked down the road to the Churchyard and planted crocus corms on Rob's grave. Lilian's lifelong love of gardening and flowers blossomed with the crocuses next Spring. The carpets of crocuses that still appear annually, either side of the path to Walton Church, were first planted by Lilian Irving, during the autumns of her childhood, as she tended the resting place of the father she never knew.

To please her grandmother, Mary Jane, she also tended the Miller's grave. As she grew older Lilian took over from Annie the yearly job of scrubbing the headstones and keeping them in pristine white condition. It was hard work.

One day, little more than a year after moving into Rose Cottage, Annie went into the small shop at the entrance to the village to stock up on supplies of sugar for her jam. The traveller, who kept the shop supplied with goods, was trying to persuade the elderly owner to invest in a large jar of sweets. She wasn't interested.

Annie thought quickly. "Excuse me," she said politely, "I'll have a jar of sweets off you. I live beside the school. If I sell this one easily, I'll have some more."

It took less than a day for every child and parent in the village to hear about those sweets. Before nightfall everybody knew. Early next morning, the first young customers were on the doorstep of Rose Cottage. Soon there were two, three and four jars of sweets to choose from.

Every morning the jars of sweets were placed on the living room table and a steady stream of eager little customers called in with their pennies and ha'pennies before school. Some of the children had to walk up to three miles from outlying cottages and their parents found that a coin to spend before school hastened them on their journey and got them to school on time! The children considered long and hard, and priced every option several times before parting with their coppers, but Annie, who understood children so well, let them take their time and made sure that they went out happy.

Walton Village School 1911. William Irving, in mourning clothes, is third from the right in the front row.

The children, with their dolly-mixtures, jelly-babies, bon-bons, palma violets, cherry-lips, gob-stoppers, liquorice sticks, nougat bars, pontefract teacakes, locust beans, sherbet dabs, troach drops, aniseed balls and sugar mice, weren't her only customers. The grown-ups started buying toffees and humbugs, barley sugars and mints.

From her first day in Rose Cottage, the small amount of money coming in had always exceeded the money going out. She looked after her pennies and, little by little, added to the money in the Post Office. The jars of sweets boosted her basic income and she invested the profits in more stock. Within another year, two things had decided their future. The elderly shopkeeper, at the entrance to the village, shut up shop and retired, leaving the way open for Annie, if she could find the space, to expand her trade – and Rose House, just behind them, became vacant.

Early in the Spring of 1914, the day before their removal from Rose Cottage to Rose House, Annie walked across the road to the school to see Mrs Bawden, the school mistress, to ask for permission to keep Will at home next day.

"My brothers are coming from the Mill to move the heavy furniture before ten o'clock, as soon as they've seen to the stock," said Annie. "I'll have to empty all the drawers and boxes and cupboards for them, and I'll need Will to help me carry it all round afterwards."

"Don't you worry Mrs Irving," said Mrs Bawden. "Just send him in for his mark on the register and then he can come home. I'll see if I can find a few helpers for you as well."

The bread was still to be baked through the night and the customers had all been asked to collect their loaves first thing in the morning. Will was duly despatched to school.

Mrs Bawden, a widow herself, had been promoted to the Headship of the thirty-two-pupil school in January, 1911. During the eighteen and a half years of her tenure she took personal responsibility for the Infant age group, realising then what many of those in High Places would take another hundred years to discover, that the Early Years are the most important in every child's life. Increasingly glowing Inspection Reports of the school confirmed her abilities. On the day that Annie moved house Mrs Bawden's assistant was not in school.

"Now then," she said, after she had called the register, "Mrs Irving is moving house today. Would anyone like to go and help her?"

Every hand in the room, from the youngest five-year-old to the oldest thirteen-year-old, shot into the air. "That's settled then," she beamed, "we'll all go."

A knock came on the door of Rose Cottage. "Good morning, Mrs Irving," said Mrs Bawden. "We've come to help you move. If it's alright with you, this is what we'll do. You go round to Rose House and direct operations there. I'll take charge here and the children will carry all the things round to you. Line up everybody!"

Lilian was three, and for the rest of her life she told and retold the story of their removal to Rose House. The sight of a steady stream of children, of all shapes and sizes, running backwards and forwards, with an amazing assortment of articles in their hands and arms, was the most vivid memory of her infancy. Mrs Bawden matched the size, weight and fragility of the items to the size and maturity of the carriers. Annie directed each item to the right room in Rose House. Nothing was packed so nothing was to be unpacked.

There were the precious jars of sweets and jams, crockery and cutlery, saucepans, kettle and jam-pan, baking tins and trays, bottles, jars and tins from their food cupboard, baking and cooking ingredients, cleaning cloths and materials, sewing box and knitting bag, towels, sheets, blankets, counterpanes, pillows and cushions, mats and curtains, buckets and bowls, a small tin bath and a wash-tub, posser, rubbing-board and flat irons, an assortment of mops and brushes, pictures and photographs, candles and oil lamp, chairs, books, toys, ornaments and clocks, and all their personal possessions and clothing.

Even at three years old, Lilian was delighted by the picture of little Billy Mounsey, the smallest and youngest child in the school, having been entrusted with her carefully folded nightdress, running excitedly from Rose Cottage to Rose House with the nightie unfolded and flapping from his out-stretched hands as though it was on a washing line.

Their mission accomplished, and a sweet of their choice in every mouth, the teacher and children returned to their classroom. When the removal men arrived from the Mill it took less than half an hour to complete the move.

Compared to Rose Cottage, Rose House was positively spacious. "There was," said Annie, "room to breathe."

The central front door opened into the right hand side of the kitchen, with a small-paned Georgian window to the left of the door. The large black-leaded grate, with its built in oven and boiler, ran the length of the left hand wall to the door that led into a smaller back-kitchen, itself leading to a small scullery, then to the wash-house from where the tiny back door opened right onto part of the village green. Everyone over four feet tall had to stoop every time they went in or out of the back door.

Further along the right hand wall of the main kitchen was the entrance to the living/dining room, or parlour, with its own Georgian window. Another door from the right hand wall of the kitchen led into a large, cool pantry with plenty of storage space. The staircase to the four bedrooms led straight up from the back of the kitchen, turned on a central landing, with one bedroom leading off, and continued up to the two front bedrooms, each with its own sash window that, upstairs, had replaced the Georgian windows. The fourth bedroom led off the far side of the landing. Each of the two smaller bedrooms had iron bedsteads ready installed that the previous tenants had found impossible to move. Thirty-six years later, when Annie moved again, those bedsteads were left where she had found them. "After all," she said, "they never really belonged to me."

There was a small front garden going right up to the back wall of Rose Cottage. To the right of the back door was a gate leading into a yard which held a good sized hen house and a shed for their coal and wood. The lavatory was in the yard as well. Although many people in the village emptied their own lavatory buckets – usually in the dark of night – Annie was one of the ones who paid the village odd-job man to undertake this task. It was Lilian's job, for as long as she could remember, to cut up newspaper into appropriate sized pieces to be strung on a nail behind the lavatory door. It was always a source of frustration for users of the facilities who chose to read the cuttings that they only ever got "half a tale." The most interesting bits always seemed to be cut off mid-story. Annie always told her children how fortunate they were to have those pieces of newspaper.

When she first went to the Mill, in 1888, they had to gather dock leaves before entering "the netty." She couldn't imagine how poor town folk of the era got on! Whenever Lilian passed a patch of frozen dock leaves in winter she counted her blessings at having been born so much later in time!

If there was more space in the new house, there was also more work. There were more rooms and windows and a staircase to clean, two fires to light and a bigger grate to blacklead weekly. The floor area downstairs, with all the scrubbing of stone slabs, was in itself a mammoth task for one small woman, who was also trying to raise her family and build up a business. The rent was higher, but she took advantage of the larger oven and baked more loaves in every batch. This meant kneading heavier lumps of dough. There was also a front garden, with its precious supply of rhubarb, blackcurrants, raspberries and gooseberries, as well as Lilian's beloved flowers, to be maintained.

Annie went to see Johnny "Toot" Little, the joiner, and asked him to build her a long table for the kitchen. The kitchen became the shop. The long table became the shop counter. It was placed just to the left of the front door and ran the length of the room. The jars of sweets took pride of place on the counter and are still mouth-wateringly remembered by older inhabitants of Walton.

Over the years, her stocks became more and more comprehensive. "You could get anything there. Groceries, green-grocery, bread and cake, stationery, picture postcards, birthday and Christmas cards, necklaces, bracelets and bangles, hair nets and slides," said one of her nieces.

Sugar, and other dried goods, was spooned out and weighed into small blue bags. The bacon was sliced by hand with an extra sharp knife, which Johnny Toot was paid to sharpen every week.

While Annie was busying herself sorting out all their belongings when they first moved in to Rose House, Lilian took herself out to play on the village green with the school children when they came out at playtime. When they went back into school she went in with them, sat herself down at a desk, and to the delight of children and teacher, joined in the lessons.

"Don't worry about her, Mrs Irving," said Mrs Bawden when Annie went to retrieve her. "She'll be alright here while you get on with your work."

When Lilian's name was added to the register, in November 1915, she had already been attending the school for almost two years.

Annie had made another investment in the Spring of 1914. She knew that Will had musical talent and that he was keenly interested in the chapel harmonium. When she heard of a second-hand piano for sale at a house outside the village, she bought it, had it installed in the parlour at Rose House and started paying for him to have piano lessons. Some of the villagers shook their heads in disbelief. What was she thinking about? A woman in her position! They feared, like the squire so long ago, that she was getting ideas above her station.

The boy, they were sure, would be better employed helping his mother with her work, than enjoying himself on that piano. But when he later mastered the chapel harmonium, and everyone benefited, they weren't quite so upset. By the time Lilian was learning to play they had forgotten their earlier worries.

5

YELLOW POOTER TO MAKE HIM GO

Mary Jane was quick to agree with Annie that the larger premises at Rose House, and the space for more stock, could benefit them both. Annie began selling potatoes, vegetables and dairy produce from the Mill, and shared the profits with her mother. More stock attracted more customers. As 1914 progressed, the future was looking more assured for the inhabitants of Rose House, but the newspaper stories were ominous.

In June, the Archduke Ferdinand of Austria was assassinated in Sarajevo and, in July, Austria and Hungary declared war on Serbia. In August, when Germany declared war on Russia and France, and then violated Belgium neutrality, Britain joined the fray and declared war on Germany. Many young men of the Brampton area answered the call to arms, took the King's shilling, and marched off to do their bit in the war that would "be over by Christmas."

Annie's brother, George Wilkinson, was quick to enlist and his farming background and knowledge of horses were soon utilised. He was assigned to the School of Farriers and spent his war years breaking-in horses and taking them to France for the army. In the south of England, John, who, perhaps as a result of his violent near-death experience in the mill-pond, held Quaker-like beliefs, was very much a pacifist. He was incarcerated in Dover Castle, as a conscientious objector, for the duration of the war. When news of his whereabouts reached Mary Jane she could only be thankful that he was too far away for the shame of it all ever to become known locally.

Rob's youngest sister, Annie Sarah, who had married a member of the Territorials in 1913, and no longer lived in the village, was one of the many young women whose husbands were called up immediately, leaving their wives to fend for themselves. Soon afterwards Annie Sarah's baby was stillborn and she herself died a few days later from puerperal fever. Her brothers, William and Abe, who rushed to her bedside from Blaydon, were convinced that simple lack of care had killed her. Life, as always in the midst of tragedy, went on.

At the village shop, Annie introduced new delights to her stock in the form of tins of cocoa. They sold well. In October, 1914, a new kettle was bought at the school for the use of school children. Eighteen children were already enjoying hot tea and cream instead of milk. Now cocoa became an added option. The charge for the cocoa was "1d per child per week until the cost of the kettle is paid."

Belgian refugees had begun to flood into England and large numbers were sent to Cumberland where they were warmly welcomed. Walton had its own refugee families and Mrs Bawden added the names of four Belgian children to the school register in January, 1915. For most of the residents of Walton this was their first experience of people from another land who didn't speak much English, but they rose to the challenge. Annie, in the village shop, became adept at communicating with her new customers who usually pointed to the items that they wanted to purchase. She was, though, somewhat at a loss when one Belgian man, whose elderly father was apparently not well, came into the shop urgently requesting, "Yellow Pooter."

Nothing that she offered was right. Eventually, in sheer frustration, the Belgian shouted, "Yellow Pooter to make him go!" Understanding dawned and the customer left triumphant with yellow liquorice powder for the relief of constipation.

The Carlisle Journal's reports on the hospitality given by local people to their Belgian guests included an account of the Annual Concert and Entertainment provided by the Committee of the Brampton Total Abstinence Society, held in the Temperance Hall on New Year's night 1915. The Town Band played and individual, local, Belgian guests were soloists. In April the Walton village school children decided to give up all their prizes that year as a "small economic sacrifice during the war."

On August 20th Mrs Bawden recorded: "Four Belgian children left school today for London. Made rapid progress since admitted. Read English Upper Readers and reached Standard IV in arithmetic." Their stay in the village had been short but memorable. Paul, a nine-year-old Belgian boy who had taken a liking to four-year-old Lilian, went to see Annie before he left to assure her, very seriously, that one day he would return and "marry Lilian." He didn't.

But, in February of that year, down the West Cumbrian Coast, in Whitehaven – the town of the terrible mining explosions that had made widows of so many women – the re-married Martha Killeen, formerly Starkey, had given birth to her fifth child, a son, at Windmill Brow. She named him Nicholas. It would be almost twenty years before the life-paths of Annie and Martha would meet.

1915 was an eventful year in other ways for Annie and her family. In April, Mrs Bawden asked her to allow Will to go, a year earlier than usual, to sit "the scholarship" at Brampton Secondary School. At that time most of the pupils at the Secondary School were fee paying, but there were some Free Places. Free Place pupils had to pay only for their books. Every year two Minor Scholarships, for children from Brampton and the surrounding villages, were also awarded.

On June 14th, 1915, Mrs Bawden noted in the school log book: "William Irving gained a Minor Scholarship to Brampton Secondary School of the value of tuition fees, books and travelling fees for his school life. He is only aged ten."

Annie was ecstatic and her reaction amazed many of her customers. At that time, most children of the area had to leave school as soon as possible to work for their families. Every summer the Education Authorities granted Exemption Notices to children still at school to allow them to work in the fields before they had reached school leaving age. The opinions that had raged over the piano lessons surfaced again, but Annie was adamant.

"My children will have the best education offered to them," she said quietly, "and I'll work every hour God sends to make it possible."

A break from the daily grind came on Monday, 23rd August. Will and Lilian left school at 11.30 so that they could enjoy an early dinner, change quickly, and then be transported with Annie, by a horse and cart from the Mill, to Brampton Junction. They were going by train to stay with Uncle Abe and Aunt Lizzie at Blaydon-on-Tyne. Their father's sister, Aunt Maggie, whom everyone had decided would be single all her life, was getting married next day, at the age of thirty-eight.

Abe and Lizzie hosted the celebrations and Annie helped with the preparations for the wedding breakfast. As George's wife was also called Lizzie, there were two "Aunt Lizzies" at the event. George's three children, Warwick, Mary and Robert were present as was their cousin Essie, daughter of their Uncle William and Aunt Polly. A good time was had by all – but little

Mary Irving, who was three at the time, always remembered how upset she had been that Essie, who was older, got a ride to the church in a carriage and she didn't!

After the reception, Maggie and her new husband, Parker Sewell, travelled back to Heads Nook in Cumberland, where they were to make their home. Annie and her children spent two nights with Abe and Lizzie and had plenty to tell Uncle Billy from the Mill when he picked them up at Brampton Junction on Wednesday.

The 6th September, 1915, was Will's first day at Secondary School. He had to walk the first mile to Walton Lane End and there catch the recently-introduced bus that would take him the further two miles into Brampton. Annie had ensured that he was freshly scrubbed and immaculately turned out in his new uniform. She was bursting with pride as she sent him on his way. She knew that something was wrong as soon as he came home. Eventually she got to the bottom of the problem.

"Can we have another sort of soap?" Will asked. "Our soap smells different from everybody else's."

Annie was mortified. She switched to the much more expensive "Knight's Castile" straight away, but it was too late. William Irving was affectionately known as "Carbolic" for the rest of his time at Brampton Secondary School.

Within a month of starting his new school, he had another problem. Someone was stealing the lunchtime sandwiches from his coat pocket. "Don't complain to the school," he begged his mother.

"Don't worry," said Annie, "we'll sort it out without bothering the school."

Next morning, Will watched fascinated as she prepared two lots of sandwiches; one lot for him and the other lot for the thief. The thief's sandwiches had slices of cheese around the edges, but in the middle was a thick paste of Colman's mustard, pepper, and the yellow liquorice powder that the Belgian refugee had found so useful. The sandwiches were duly stolen and Annie made a second batch the next day. She needn't have bothered. The thief, whoever he was, had lost his appetite for Will's lunch. There were no more sandwiches stolen from his coat pocket.

The only other upset of his Secondary Education came when he managed to tear a hole in his school trousers. A replacement pair would not be cheap. Annie was sure that she would be able to darn the hole and that nobody would notice.

All went well until Will bent down to pick up a pencil that he had dropped. "Look," yelled one of his classmates, "Carbolic's got a carbuncle on his arse."

"It's a sock," shouted another, looking more closely at the darn. Annie found the money for the new trousers.

The schools, in the Brampton area, during the war years, were often forced to close. Sometimes this was due to the weather, but most often it was to prevent the spread of infectious diseases. Closures of up to four weeks were common, in Walton, for influenza, whooping-cough, mumps, measles and even an "epidemic of sore throats." Childhood still a precarious business with outbreaks of many life-threatening illnesses. Even with all her experience of tending the sick. Annie was often exhausted with nursing her children while trying to earn her living and keep the home running. Lilian, particularly, was not a robust child and always seemed to be going down with something. Their recovery from every infection was a great relief and regarded by Annie as "prayers answered."

In Preston, her elder brother, policeman Jim Blenkinsop and his wife, "Preston Annie," had been less fortunate. They had suffered the loss of each of their two eldest children, Annie and Leslie, before their second birthdays, with illnesses that had begun with sore throats. A few years later they were further devastated by the death of their daughter, Margaret, with peritonitis following abdominal surgery. A broken-hearted nurse from the hospital came to see them, following their bereavement, to tell them that she thought they should know that the peritonitis had been caused by a dressing not having been removed after the operation. Unwilling to compromise the nurse, Jim and his wife, although inconsolable, let the matter drop. Their youngest child, Eric, survived and eventually joined his father in the Lancashire Police Force where, like his father, he reached the rank of Inspector.

The Brampton and District Medical Officer, Dr Morrison and later, Dr Arnott, always took the decision, when infectious outbreaks occurred, to close the school at Walton and the message was relayed by telegram or "wire." There was no telephone at the school and all communication with both the Medical Officer and the Education Authorities had to go via the village Post Office. Confidentiality was not easy to maintain and everybody knew the school's business very quickly. Annie, in the village shop, knew what was going on at the school almost before the Head teacher herself. Letters to parents were never necessary with such a grapevine in existence.

Whenever the school was reopened after a closure, Mrs Bawden found that she had to do a lot of revision work as so much had been forgotten during the long closures. When the school reopened on 29th January, 1916, only twenty-eight children were present. Jeannie Calvert was still ill with chicken-pox, Alfred Brown had had an accident to his hand, and John Little was tending sheep! Delivering the curriculum seems to have been just as big a headache as it is today.

Mrs Bawden lived with her sister at Ridgevale Terrace in Brampton. She drove a pony and trap and the pony was usually tethered on the village green during school hours. In the exceptional year of 1915 she was forced to close the school on 19th March "owing to huge snowdrifts not cut through until 2.00 p.m. in the afternoon. In driving home previous evening had to be dug out." Again, in December of that year, the school had to be closed because of the "very dangerous state of the roads."

Summer treats for the school children were provided annually by the Johnsons at Castlesteads. Mrs Johnson was a regular visitor to the school and took a keen interest in all its activities. She particularly encouraged the children in their war efforts. In 1914 the children gave a Christmas concert at the school which was attended by most of the village, with proceeds going to the Walton Nursing Association and comforts for soldiers and sailors. Four pounds five shillings and sixpence was realised. Everyone was very patriotic. The school was always decorated and Union Jacks hoisted for Empire Day on 24th May. St. Michael's Hospital, on Longtown Road at Brampton, where wounded soldiers were sent to recuperate, received regular gifts from the Walton school children. On one occasion sixteen teaspoons were given for the use of soldiers. In March, 1918, the children went round the village and its surrounding hamlets, and collected 318 eggs for the wounded at the hospital.

The next month, April, saw the end of an era in Walton with the death of the Squire. Mrs Bawden recorded: "It is with the deepest regret that I enter the death of Mr. T.P. Johnson JP, Chairman of School Managers and our most valued Trustee." His son succeeded him at Castlesteads. Eight days later, Mrs Johnson gave the school permission to buy a new kettle for the children's cocoa. They had burnt the bottom out of the old one.

Annie, like the other women of the village, had her own part to play in the War Effort and the supporting of the troops. Every spare minute was spent in the knitting of socks, of which there was apparently a great shortage, for soldiers.

Food, although scarce in the towns and cities during the war years, was not the same problem for country dwellers. They all had their own gardens for growing vegetables, the fruits of the hedgerows for jams and pies, mushrooms in the fields, fish in the rivers, and an abundance of wild rabbits for meat. Her brothers at the Mill kept Annie supplied with as many rabbits as she needed, both for herself and her customers. If a game bird strayed across their path all country folk knew how to despatch it quickly and take it home for a feast. Farm produce was also available.

Annie was one of the many who kept her own poultry. Every spring she had a broody hen hatching and rearing chicks in her back yard. Bread was not rationed until February, 1917, and the rationing did not affect her trade. The food supplies nationally, however, were dwindling and, in the autumn of 1918, as the war was drawing to a close, The Ministry of Food directed the teachers in the country schools to abandon their lessons and take all the children blackberry picking for the Nation. On the 6th September, Mrs Bawden despatched thirty-nine and a half pounds of brambles collected by the children. A further fifty-one pounds were sent four days later "collected in the evenings by order of the Ministry of Food."

In October, the month before Germany signed an armistice with the allies, the world-wide influenza pandemic reached Britain. In Blaydon-on-Tyne, George Irving's wife, Lizzie, now the mother of five children – the youngest still a baby – was one of the twenty-five million who lost their lives. Lizzie's youngest sister, sixteen-year-old Jane, was sent to help the bereaved family, until such time as an older sister, Rachel, could be freed from her "in-service" contract to take over the responsibility. Annie and her children's trip to Blaydon on this occasion was very different from their last visit.

For seven-year-old Mary Irving, the loss of her mother was compounded by having to wear only black clothes for a year. She hated being so conspicuous and felt even more "different" from her classmates. Abe and his wife, the other Lizzie, who had lost their own baby son five years previously, and would never be able to have more children, wanted to adopt George's five-year-old son, Robert, but it was decided that this was not a good idea. They contented themselves by giving as much practical help as they could to George and his young family.

Annie, who attended all the Saturday morning Jumble Sales in Walton and the surrounding areas, and secured many bargains, always found clothes for George's family as well as her own. She regularly posted parcels of children's clothes to Blaydon, where the quality of Jumble Sale stock was not so good. In the Brampton district, the more affluent people saw it as their duty to donate generously of their, often little used, clothing for the benefit of good causes and the area's poor. Annie took full advantage of their generosity. She would hear of forthcoming Jumble Sales from her ever-growing number of customers and, leaving Will and Lilian in charge of the shop, set off in search of bargains. Walks of up to five miles were common.

As well as the Jumble Sales, there were often Country House and Farm Sales to be attended, where all the furnishings and equipment were generally sold at knock-down prices. It was at one of these Sales, in 1919, that Annie picked up her greatest bargain – a bike! She pushed it home triumphantly and was greeted with shouts of joy from Will and Lilian. That bike was to transform their lives, although Annie herself never rode it.

Both Will and Lilian became experts in bicycle maintenance, the fixing of chains and repairing of punctures, while Annie added puncture repair kits to her stock. They devised a system of sharing the bike if they both wanted to go to Brampton, or elsewhere, at the same time. One of them would ride the bike for about 200 yards and then prop it against the hedge and start walking. The other would then walk up, collect the bike, and go riding past the walker for another two hundred yards before, in turn, propping it against the hedge. Journey times were considerably reduced.

For many widowed mothers (and fathers) of Annie's generation, re-marriage was still, as it had been for centuries, the only practical solution for those without regular income. There were no State benefits of any kind. Annie had witnessed, both in the village and in Newcastle, the penalising of the children of the first marriage that was so often the result of such an escape route. She was determined that, whatever the personal cost, re-marriage for her would never be an option. She had made up her mind as Rob lay dying and never changed it. Life wasn't easy, she later explained, but she was mistress of her own destiny ("and purse") and she had her memories. She learned very quickly to be reserved in her manner to male customers so that no false messages were transmitted. Widowers and single men who, over the years, came calling in surprising numbers, were politely thanked and gently refused. Some of the married men, whose intentions were definitely not honourable, received sharper treatment.

One persistent man who, she claimed, didn't understand the word "No," got into the habit of knocking on her door late at night, on his way home from the Black Bull. One hot, dry, summer night as he stood beneath her bedroom window, protesting his undying affection, she flung open the sash window and emptied the contents of a ready prepared, very full, bucket of cold water over his head.

"That'll cool you down," she said grimly, "now get away home to your wife." As he squelched off she called, "And think yourself lucky that it wasn't the chamber pot I tipped over you."

She went back to bed and laughed joyously to herself as she wondered how he would explain his saturated condition to his wife.

"Cold water was always the best treatment for dogs on heat," she said, when recounting the tale to her grandchildren.

She often railed against the morals of the era that had different standards for men than those expected of women. She was particularly bitter about one local farming family whose wayward son "left offspring all over the district" without rebuke, but whose daughter, on producing an illegitimate child, was reduced to the position of a skivvy. The young woman was never allowed to leave the farm again during her parents' lifetime. When visitors called she had to vacate the rooms where they were entertained. The Workhouse would have been her only alternative.

Another young woman, who married the father of her expected child, was still, on her father's instructions, rejected by her family. She had a second child just after her husband was sent to fight in the war. Even when he was killed in action, her father refused to acknowledge or help her. On days when he was away from home, her mother and brother loaded up a cart with coal and provisions, and delivered them to her surreptitiously.

"I wouldn't have been able to serve the old devil if he'd ever come in the shop," said Annie.

6

SCHOLARSHIP AND SCARLET FEVER

Rose House was very much of its time in its furnishing and decoration. The front parlour, although small, had large family portraits adorning its walls with Annie and Rob's wedding photograph taking pride of place. Religious texts and homilies were everywhere displayed. "If I can help somebody, as I pass along life's way, then my journey will not be in vain," was given a prominent position. In the bedrooms, the biblical texts were ornately framed and large pictures hung over the beds. The much treasured "Good Samaritan" was over Annie's own bed.

For most of the time there were at least two mattresses on her brass bedstead. She put any mattresses, not in current use, underneath her own feather bed to keep them aired. Whenever visitors were expected the front guest bedroom mattress was returned to its mahogany bedstead and warmed with stone hot-water bottles to ensure the comfort of the visitors. In later life, when she was the only permanent resident of Rose House, she had to "climb a mountain" to get into bed. No visitors to her home ever "got damp in their bones," and her grandchildren saw nothing unbelievable in the story of "The Princess and the Pea."

As well as all the biblical texts that surrounded them, and influenced them for life, in Rose House, Annie had a vast array of proverbs, learned as a child at school, from which she never failed to select and repeat according to the situation in which they found themselves. "Many hands make light work" and "Too many cooks spoil the broth" were cheerfully used with equal frequency.

The table in the parlour was covered with a red chenille cloth and had an oil lamp as its centre-piece. All Will's and Lilian's homework was done at this table. The "Press," a large walnut cupboard with drawers underneath, held all the linen, crockery and china. Besides the obligatory aspidistra on a stand, there were vivid red geraniums in pots on the window-sill. One stunning white geranium stood in the middle. The geraniums were allowed to grow to the height of the window and always seemed to be in glorious full bloom.

As well as space for the piano, in a corner near the window, room had to be found for the large frame that held the hessian for the making of mats. There was always a new mat on the go. The mats were of two types, "hookies" and "stobbies." The "stobbies" were made of small rectangular strips of cloth that were bodged, individually, and close together, into the hessian. Lilian preferred the "hookies" as they were made from long strips of material rolled into a ball and hooked in and out of the hessian at a much faster pace than could be achieved with "stobbies."

On her Jumble Sale outings Annie usually managed to acquire plenty of cheap items, no longer fit for wear, that could be washed and cut up for the production of beautiful mats. As she grew older Lilian would create ever more intricate designs for the mats that she then drew onto the hessian. All the mats had to be taken outside and shaken vigorously on cleaning days. The stone floors, downstairs, were scrubbed with hot water and carbolic soap. The parlour and the bedrooms eventually had the luxury of linoleum underneath the mats. Furniture was polished, grates black-leaded, brasses cleaned and windows washed every Friday. The scrubbing out of the lavatory was another Friday job. This particular job revealed all of the Pollyanna philosophies that were so much a part of Annie's make-up as she counted her blessings with, "I'm glad I never had to scrub out, or use, the lavatories in some of those old farm-houses in Castle Carrock. They had great long wooden seats, with holes of different sizes all along them, so that whole families could use them at the same time."

Housework was kept "on top of" by allocating specific extra tasks to each week-day. Monday was for washing, Tuesday for ironing, Wednesday for the bottoming of bedrooms and Thursday for the home-baking of cakes and pastries.

An unwritten law decreed that all housework should be completed in the morning. "Respectable" women washed, changed from working clothes and apron into "afternoon" clothes, and generally made themselves presentable after the clearing away of the 12.00 p.m. dinner dishes.

Annie baked bread "for the village" six days a week. For many years she got up at 4.00 a.m. to ensure that all the loaves were kneaded and baked in good time. Her profit margins were low, but guaranteed, and money so dearly earned was never wasted. When Lilian came in to say that she had lost a sixpence on the village green she was immediately sent back out "to find it." Matt Ridley, who listened to her tale of woe as she surveyed the expanse of grass, offered to help with the search and "found" the sixpence in minutes. Annie later returned the coin and thanked him for his thoughtfulness, but, "If we're to survive decently, my children have to learn the value of money," she said.

Her washing was possed in a dolly-tub and wrung by hand or in a large mangle with wooden rollers. Once she was established in Rose House, she purchased large water-butts for the corners of the house and used the water they collected for her washing. On wet days it was hung to dry on clothes horses set around the parlour fire. Freezing winter days would see sheets and towels being brought in from the washing line "by the yard, like boards."

Spring Cleaning was a mammoth annual chore. Starting upstairs, every room was completely turned out. Windows were flung open. Curtains, covers, blankets and counterpanes were all washed and dried in the sun outside. Ceilings were whitened and walls washed down or re-papered. Mattresses were turned and aired outside in the sun. Bedsteads were washed. Wardrobes, chests, cupboards and drawers were emptied and re-lined. No brazen moth, spider or beetle could be left undisturbed. Mats were hung on the washing line and attacked with carpet beaters. Every item of crockery and china was thoroughly washed and safely re-stored.

Downstairs, the chimneys were swept before cleaning commenced. Everything in the rooms was covered with dust cloths before the Sweep arrived. Spring cleaning the shop and pantry was no easy task with every precious item having to be moved and checked while still maintaining the service to customers. While her children were young, Annie paid a neighbour to help her with the spring cleaning. One year, while papering the spare bedroom, the neighbour came across a hole in the wall and, without further ado, stuffed Lilian's rag doll into the hole and papered over it before Annie knew what was happening. Lilian never got over it. Every night when she went to bed she thought about "poor Mary-Ann behind the paper."

"It's a good job you weren't there, Sponger," she told their pampered ginger tomcat, "or she might have stuffed you in the wall."

Sponger lived contentedly at Rose House for seventeen years. As a kitten he was pushed happily around the village in a doll's pram, giving Bel Ridley, "quite a turn," the first time she saw his furry ginger face underneath the baby's bonnet when she stopped to admire Lilian's "baby." Sponger kept the mice away from the shop and was well fed and cherished for his efforts.

Lilian and Hemp under the apple tree.

Lilian's dog, Hemp, was never really her dog at all. A black and tan border collie, who belonged to George and Ellen Watson in the White House at the end of the village, he and Lilian found each other on the village green when he was a puppy. Kind-hearted George Watson accepted the inevitable and made a "pact" with Lilian that was somehow communicated to the dog. Hemp trotted down the village to Lilian every morning for almost twenty years, lay down in the shop to be fussed by customers during the day, and trotted back home at night for dinner and bed.

"You could set your clock by Old Hemp," said the villagers who saw him pass.

The end of the war years saw great changes in the country as soldiers began to return from the battle-fields to a "land fit for heroes." As a reward for their war efforts, women over thirty were given the vote in 1918. Men, still regarded as superior beings, could vote at twenty-one. The general euphoria would be short-lived. Country areas saw an increase in the number of tramps, many of them displaced soldiers looking for casual work, sleeping in barns, and knocking on doors at meal times to politely request a share of the food. Annie never refused these requests.

Years later she heard how, in Whitehaven, one of Martha Killeen's sisters, who had remarried a few years after receiving her black-edged telegram from the War Office, was in the kitchen with her new husband and baby, when the soldier who had been reported "killed in action" walked through the door. He took one look at the domestic scene and stricken faces in front of him, turned on his heel, and walked back out. He was never seen again. His story was not uncommon.

In Brampton, the people decided that their War Memorial should be a Cottage Hospital that would benefit the whole district. It was a project that received massive popular support and fund raising began in earnest. The foundation stones were laid in 1920.

At Walton Mill, weddings were in the air. Annie's brother Billy started the ball rolling in 1919 with his marriage to farmer's daughter Sally Jardine. They set up home at Hallburn Croft Farm, Longtown, next to Sally's parents at Hallburn, moving later to The Height near Wigton. Mary Jane's youngest son, Bob, was left to take over the running of the Mill. Bob had been planning to emigrate to New Zealand, but Billy's marriage put a stop to that idea as Mary Jane told him very clearly where his duties lay.

In April, 1920, there was a big double wedding at the Mill when Mary married Fred Edgar and Lil married Dick Jardine, brother of Billy's wife Sally. It was standing room only for all the guests that tried to pack themselves into the chapel. Mary and Fred made their home in the village of Cargo. Lil and Dick started married life with Dick's parents at Hallburn, before going to farm at Ghyllhead, Wigton.

In May, just as they were getting over the excitement of the double wedding and plans were being made for Kate's wedding to Peter Graham in October, Annie got a letter in the post from Mr Cousins, Will's Headmaster. The letter asked if she would be able to come to see him, at a time of her own choosing, as there were confidential matters that he would like to discuss with her. Annie couldn't imagine what it was all about. She ran across the road to the school and showed the letter to Mrs Bawden, who was equally at a loss.

"The best thing you can do Mrs Irving," she said, "is close the shop for a few hours and go into Brampton to see what's going on. You won't rest till you know."

Annie went home to wash and change into her Sunday Best. She added her best coat, hat, shoes and gloves – "You could always tell a lady by her shoes and gloves" – walked down to the Lane End and caught the bus into Brampton. She went nervously into the school and was shown immediately into the Head's office. Someone brought her a cup of tea and Mr Cousins introduced her to the Senior Science master, who also wanted to see her.

"We were wondering, Mrs Irving," said Mr Cousins, "what do you intend to do with Will?"

"Do with him?" asked Annie. "I don't really know. I was hoping that after he got his School Certificate and matriculated he'd be able to get a good job."

"The thing is, Mrs Irving," said the Science master, "your son has a first class brain. It would be a terrible waste to put him in some dead-end office job."

"He desperately wants to be a doctor," said Mr Cousins, "but he doesn't think he can ask you to support him for so long. He knows how hard it has been for you already."

"A doctor!" exclaimed Annie. "I'll never be able to pay for him to be a doctor."

"You won't have to," explained Mr Cousins. "We are sure that if HE works hard and WE work hard, he'll get a scholarship. But he will need you to maintain him until he's qualified. Are you prepared to do that for him, Mrs Irving? We do realise what we are asking of you."

They both looked at her. Annie took a deep breath.

"I'll do it," she said. "We've never starved in winter yet. I'll manage it somehow."

"You're a remarkable woman, Mrs Irving," said Mr Cousins. "You can rest assured that we'll do our part."

Annie walked out of the school in a daze. She saved the cost of the bus fare to the Lane End and walked the three miles back to Walton.

"It's belt tightening time again," she said to herself as she headed for home. She went straight into the school to tell Mrs Bawden what she had let herself in for.

"You'll never regret it," Mrs Bawden told her.

"We're going to have a doctor in the house then, are we?" she asked Will when he came home from school. "I don't know what the village will have to say about it when they find out." They said plenty.

When Will went back to school after the Summer holidays to begin studying for his Highers and the Scholarship exam that would decide his future, he was one of only two pupils in the sixth form.

"There's Annie Irving working herself to death to keep that great healthy lad with his nose in a book," was the general opinion, "and when he comes out to walk round the village you can see he's in a world of his own. Too much book reading addles the brain!" It didn't.

After Kate's wedding in October, and the settling in of the newly married couple at the Dove Cote Farm at Walton, Bob, who wasn't going to let Mary Jane have everything her own way at the Mill, announced that he was marrying Edie, from neighbouring Low Rigg farm, in November, and bringing her home to live at the Mill. Mary Jane was flabbergasted. She had been mistress in her own kitchen for fifty years, since she was eighteen, and she wasn't going to make way easily. There were storms ahead for Bob and Edie.

Annie had a new worry of her own that November. She had taken Lilian into Carlisle to choose a present for her tenth birthday. Within days it was obvious that, once again, Lilian was "going down with something."

"Call in and ask Dr Nicholson to come out on your way to school," Annie told Will. "I've had a terrible night with her."

Dr Nicholson had a surgery at the bottom of Gelt Road in Brampton and he came straight out to Walton. "It's Scarlet Fever, Mrs Irving," he said. "I'll have to get her into the Isolation Hospital right away."

Annie thought she would collapse. "You can't do that," she said. "As soon as word gets out I'll be ruined. Nobody will come in the shop for months and we'll all end up in the Workhouse."

"It's the law, Mrs Irving," said the doctor, "I'll be in terrible trouble myself if there's an epidemic and I haven't reported this case."

"Just tell me what I need to do to keep her here," begged Annie. "I'll do everything you tell me."

Dr Nicholson had known Annie for years. He was the one, by his conversations with Will, who had first inspired him to be a doctor. He looked at her and said quietly, "Alright, Mrs Irving. I'll be back in less than an hour. As soon as I've gone, take off all the clothes you're wearing now and leave them in a bucket of disinfectant outside Lilian's bedroom door. Wash your hands and arms in carbolic soap and don't go back in the room till I get back. You'll have to inform the school, but don't tell another soul what's wrong with her."

Once again, Annie ran across the road to see Mrs Bawden and told her the terrible news.

"I'll have to write it in the log book," said Mrs Bawden, "but nobody ever bothers to read it and they won't hear it from me."

Her entry for the 21st November simply said, "One child being nursed at home with Scarlet Fever."

Within an hour the wonderful Dr Nicholson was walking into Rose House with a huge pile of overalls, a curtain to be saturated in disinfectant and hung across Lilian's bedroom door, and a large quantity of all the carbolic disinfectant that Annie would need.

"She mustn't come out of that room for four weeks," he told Annie, "and nobody, other than yourself, can go in. Put on a clean overall every time you go into the room. Keep a bucket of

disinfectant and a bowl of clean water and carbolic soap outside
the door. Put the overall in the bucket every time you come out
and scrub your hands and arms. When she's better, everything
that has been in the room with her will have to be burned. The
wallpaper will have to be stripped and burned and the room
fumigated."

"I'll do it," said Annie. "I'll never be able to thank you enough."

The next four weeks were horrendous. Lilian was in the room
leading off the first landing. She understood that she must not
cry out for anything while customers' voices could be heard in
the shop. Annie ran upstairs between customers, sometimes just
to call through the door, to ensure that she was alright. The
customers, who eventually realised Lilian was ill, were told that
she had 'flu'. Anyone who wanted to "pop up and see her" was
told, "she's asleep at the moment."

"You don't look very well yourself, Annie," many people
commented.

It was no wonder. Annie had never been so exhausted at any
other time in her life. As soon as the shop was locked at night,
she was boiling, possing and mangling, overalls, sheets, towels,
and nightdresses, and drying them around the parlour fire, which
had to be kept going around the clock. She tried to get an
hour's sleep before starting on the bread baking, but Lilian
seemed to need even more nursing through the night than in the
daytime. Because of the necessity to maintain absolute secrecy,
she couldn't ask any of the family to help her. She herself, Mrs
Bawden, Will, and, of course Lilian, kept the secret for over
twenty-five years and then "the next generation" heard all about
it. When the four weeks were up, Lilian was finally allowed out
of the bedroom. She was stripped and washed, dressed in clean

clothes, and moved into Annie's room.

"It's a bit late for Guy Fawkes Day," called passing villagers as they saw Annie's massive bonfire, with a mattress in the middle.

She stripped the wallpaper, fumigated the room, and re-papered, during the next few nights. It was all finished in time for Christmas. Nobody else in the village caught Scarlet Fever.

Life was hard for the new bride at Walton Mill. Mary Jane, her mother-in-law, took a dominant role from the start and supervised her unmercifully.

"Make sure you dust down the sides," she instructed, as Edie approached the sideboard with a duster.

At Low Rigg, Edie had been used to putting plenty of butter aside for the family's use before sending the rest to market. "How many pounds of butter do I keep back?" she asked Mary Jane.

"One!" replied Mary Jane severely. "You'll have to watch her," she told Bob, "she's extravagant."

By February, in 1921, Edie was getting desperate. She couldn't even "mix a pudding" without interference. "If you don't do something, that old woman's going to break that lass's heart," one of his hired men told Bob.

Bob went to see Annie to tell her of the misery Mary Jane was causing at the Mill.

"Leave it to me, Bob," she said. "I'll have a word with her next time she comes in the shop."

Annie valued her independence but she had to do something about her mother. She knew exactly which buttons to press.

"I've been meaning to ask you," she said, when Mary Jane came to tell her about Edie's failings, "would you consider coming to live with me? There's plenty of room. I've got so much work to do in the shop, I just don't know how I'm going to get through the Spring Cleaning. You could take charge of the house and I could run the shop and do all the heavy work."

Mary Jane's face lit up. "I'll think about it," she said. "If I do come, I'll pay my way. I'm still getting the rent from Castle Carrock."

She went straight up to her bedroom without speaking when she got back to the Mill. An hour later she came down with her belongings packed in a bag.

"I'm off to live with Annie," she announced. "You can drop my chest off in the cart later."

She marched off to Rose House, swinging her bag, as she had done fifty years earlier on the way from Gretna to Castle Carrock. It was quite a bit heavier this time and her pace wasn't nearly so brisk.

She had brought with her all the old Blenkinsop wills and documents from Castle Carrock, which she deposited in the cupboard of Annie's wash-stand. They would be stored safely there for another eighty years – and move house four times – before one of her great-granddaughters would unearth them and become fascinated by their contents.

When she moved into Rose House, Mary Jane already had seven surviving grandchildren. Besides Will and Lilian, there were Tom and Betty (now grown up) in Ontario; Eric at Preston; and Archie and Walton, sons of George and Sally Wilkinson at Felling-on-Tyne.

With all the recent weddings – only John was still single – the numbers of Mary Jane's grandchildren would more than double in the next five years. Eventually they would almost treble. To begin with, Mary Lilian ("little Lily"), Bill and George Edgar were born at Cargo. Jardine Wilkinson was born at Hallburn Croft, before Billy and Sally took over The Height. Lil and Dick Jardine had another Mary and then Tom at Ghyllhead; and a new generation began at the Mill with the births of Edna and yet another Tom.

Childbirth was still a dangerous and life-threatening event. New mothers, who had been safely delivered, always went to Church to give thanks for their survival of the ordeal. They were not allowed to mix with society until they had been "churched."

Mary Jane's whole family were completely devastated when, in February 1922, after a doctor was eventually called to the complications that arose at the birth of Kate's first baby, he asked her traumatised husband, "Have I to save the mother or the baby? I can't save them both."

"The mother," was Peter's immediate response.

Their "perfect" baby son died at birth and was not allowed a burial in consecrated ground. Early next morning, just as dawn was trying to break, in a damp grey mist, Annie and Mary Jane went with Peter for the short ceremony and burial of the tiny coffin, in the place reserved for such occasions, just behind the wall in Walton churchyard. The grief was unbearable. The sun did follow the rain. Kate and Peter's daughter, Muriel, was safely delivered in their new farm at Swainsteads, in the Spring of 1925. Muriel would always be "special" to them all.

Lilian was especially delighted with all the new additions to the family, who were all regular visitors to Rose House. It became the focal point and meeting place for the extended family. They formed a central support network for each other, the links of which would be stretched and expanded over the years, but never broken. "Little Lily" Edgar was, reputedly, the liveliest of the new batch of grandchildren. She enchanted them all with her sparkling personality and nobody sat down for very long when she came to visit.

Lily was born in May, 1921. Mary Jane was now comfortably settled into Rose House. Her Victorian brass candlesticks, her brass candle-snuffers, and the Staffordshire Clay ornaments from Castle Carrock were all placed on the parlour mantel-piece. The settling-in was not without incident as she tried to establish her position and organise them all into her ways.

"It's no wonder you can't get your work done," she told Annie. "You spend too much time talking to customers."

"If I didn't talk to them, they wouldn't come in the shop," Annie retorted. "You look after your jobs in your way, and I'll look after mine in my way."

Looking after the shop and catering for the needs of different customers was an art in itself. The ordering of perishable goods had to be very carefully managed. Some people preferred to buy "little and often" and live from hand to mouth. Others liked to keep well-stocked pantries. There was usually at least one person who would arrive at Rose House on a Sunday afternoon desperately pleading for a tin of salmon, corned beef or fruit, to cater for unexpected visitors. Annie would never accept the money for such items before Monday morning. Village people, however, were honest and she was never left out of pocket by her last-minute customers. During the week, everyone who came into the shop liked to pass the time of day and catch up with village news. Troubles and joys were shared in equal measure. It was surprising how often someone beset by worries would suddenly need to purchase a small item from the shop and take the opportunity to talk through their problems with a sympathetic listener. Although she would give practical advice where she could, listening was often all that Annie could do. Confidences were never betrayed.

Everybody knew everybody else for miles around. When, one day, a smartly dressed woman, accompanied by her daughter, drew up in a pony and trap and came into the shop with a very long shopping list, Annie couldn't help wondering where she had come from. The story of renting a house outside the village was noticeably vague. Annie dutifully filled the shopping bags lined up on the counter and totalled up the cost.

"Thank you very much," said the woman. "Now I'll send a man round to pay you later."

"Oh no you won't," said Annie, and she emptied the shopping bags quicker than she had filled them.

"How dare you?" screeched the customer. "Who do you think you are?"

"My name is on the wall outside," said Annie. "I'm Annie Irving and I don't know you from Adam. So be off with you."

The women flounced out empty handed. A few weeks later Annie had a visit from the Police in Brampton. Two women had been going round the shops in the outlying villages, filling their bags, and leaving heavily laden without paying. Who they were, and where they came from, was never discovered.

The living arrangements with her mother at Rose House worked reasonably well, but the stress levels, as always with Mary Jane in residence, were often high. Kate and Lil, who each had spare rooms, made sure that they took their share of the responsibility. Eventually, Mary Jane went to Kate for a month every Spring and to Lil every Autumn. She also went to Billy, at the Height, for her "summer holidays," and left Sally, his wife, "exhausted."

After the war many landowners sold off some of their tenant farms and Castlesteads was no exception. Bob and Edie bought Walton Mill in the summer of 1921. Although Bob continued to crush oats and work the Saw Mill, flour production ceased. By the time his daughter Edna was born, later in the year, the large millstone, that had ground flour for centuries, was redundant.

1921 was also the year that Lady Rosalind, the much loved and respected Countess of Carlisle, died. The people of the Brampton district wanted to erect a memorial to remember the contribution that she and her late husband, the ninth Earl, had made to the area. In 1930, a stone memorial shelter, dedicated to the Earl and his Countess, was erected on the Sands at Brampton. The shelter was built in the shape of a gin house at Burtholme that was used as a shelter for a horse to walk round as it turned the shaft that powered farm machinery. The millstone from Walton Mill formed the centre-piece of the roof.

The Sands is an open grassed area, forking out into a large triangle on Brampton's Eastern fringe. It was given to the first parish council by the Earl of Carlisle in 1895, and had been the scene of fairs and celebrations for hundreds of years. The "middle road," running through the centre of the Sands, was a favourite walking area for courting couples at the turn of the century, and the main road to Newcastle. The road to the left of the triangle goes to Lanercost and the right hand road leads to Alston.

The millstone on the shelter on the Sands at Brampton.

Everyone connected with Walton Mill was delighted with the honour bestowed on their old millstone.

"I've watched that go round a good few times," Annie would comment every time she passed the stone on the shelter.

7

DANCING ON THE VILLAGE GREEN

Lilian got her Minor Scholarship to Brampton Secondary School in 1922, when she was eleven. She was the third child during Mrs Bawden's time as Headteacher of the small village school to achieve this success. Over the years, a number of children had also obtained Free Places. The Education Authorities decided to recognise the school's achievement with a special ceremony on the 21st July. Annie and Mary Jane joined other villagers in the celebrations and Mrs Bawden recorded, "Lilian Mary Irving received Roll of Honour on behalf of ten pupils who had won Free Places and Minor Scholarships at Brampton Secondary School. A 'Red Letter Day' for our school."

The main highlight of 1922, however, was the news that Will, at only seventeen years of age, had won his scholarship to the University of Durham College of Medicine, and would be able to begin his training a year earlier than was normally allowed. There was great rejoicing at Rose House and heartfelt congratulations from everyone who came into the shop.

News of his intentions reached Castlesteads. One morning, as Mary Jane sat on a chair outside the front garden, a pony and trap stopped beside Rose House. The driver remained in his seat, but his passenger, the governess from Castlesteads, alighted and marched into the shop.

"Good morning," said Annie, somewhat taken aback by the figure in front of her.

"Now, Mrs Irving," said the governess haughtily, without returning her greeting, "I've come to tell you that the Squire is not happy with you."

"Isn't he indeed," asked Annie, "and what have I done to upset the Squire?"

"He has heard," continued the governess, "that you are forgetting who you are. He wants to remind you that you are a village shopkeeper and shopkeepers' sons do not rise above themselves to think they can be doctors."

"It's nothing to do with the Squire," said Annie indignantly. "I'm not asking him for his help or his opinion."

"The Squire has told me to tell you," kept on the governess, twitching her nose, "that Dr Arnott's son wants to be a doctor and he is having great difficulty passing the entrance exams. How dare you have the temerity to think that you, a village woman, can ever get her son to mix with his betters?"

"Get out of my shop," shouted Annie furiously, grabbing the sweeping brush that was so conveniently to hand, "and don't ever come back. When you get back to Castlesteads you can tell the Squire that I know nothing about Dr Arnott's son, but MY son passed those exams with honours, and MY son is going to be a doctor whether the Squire likes it or not."

Mary Jane outside Rose House.

Calling, "Get off with you! Go on, get off with you!" Annie began sweeping the brush vigorously in the direction of the governess, who turned sharply round and scuttled out of the shop. She broke into a run on the path outside and jumped frantically into the trap, Annie's brush dusting her heels.

"You've done it this time," said Mary Jane, as Annie stood beside her, arms akimbo, brush still clutched in her right hand, watching the pony and trap racing out of the village.

"She stormed in here, with her grey skirts rustling and billowing, like a galleon in full sail," Annie frequently recalled. "But I swept her out like a dog, with its tail between its legs." Mary Jane and Lilian were left in charge of the shop on the day that Annie and Will travelled to Durham, for Will to become better acquainted with the University, and for Annie to meet his future landlady. She took an immediate liking to the landlady, "a decent hard-working woman," who looked after her until Will was ready to go home. Over several cups of tea, and exchanges of life-stories, they easily reached a friendly agreement on the payment for his lodgings.

Only the early part of his course, however, was based in Durham. Most of his training was at Kings College Newcastle and meant a change of digs. For a time he lodged with Abe and Lizzie at Blaydon before joining a fellow student in lodgings in Newcastle.

The other student had been brought up to think that it was good manners never to clear one's plate at meal times. The landlady believed in "waste not want not" and kept reducing the sizes of their portions to match the needs of the polite lodger. When he was down to half a slice of bread for his ration Will, who became "Bill" when he went to Durham, reached an agreement with the landlady. He ate with his fellow student in the dining room and then went into the kitchen to have the other half of his dinner with the landlady.

Tuition fees were all covered by his scholarship and there were systems in place that gave extra cash prizes to the students who achieved the highest marks in their end of year exams. The cash prizes helped to cover the cost of extra books and clothing, and relieved the financial pressure on hard-pressed families.

During his five years of training Bill would be an outstanding student. He would win the Dickinson, the Charlton and the Philipson scholarships, and the class prize in medicine and therapeutics. He would also get the silver medal in anatomy and become gold medallist of his year. All of this success, however, was still to come, and Annie had to plan all their expenses without any expectations of extra help.

At the same time that Bill was going to Durham, Lilian had to be equipped for the Secondary School. Conveniently, the bike, on which he had cycled to school every day since its purchase, was now available for Lilian. She didn't have to wait at the Lane End for the bus.

Bill's suitcase for Durham was strapped to the bike and Lilian went with him to Brampton Junction to see him off when the great day arrived. In their well-practiced fashion they took turns walking and riding. This method of transport was used at the beginning and end of every term for the next five years. One term end there were two suitcases and Bill wouldn't tell her what was in the second case until they got back to Rose House. The case contained a medical skeleton – of human bones, not replicas. His landlady had become nervous about entering his room with the skeleton in residence, so it came to sit on a chair in the guest bedroom at Rose House. They put a bowler hat on his head and called him Boris.

Whenever the Blaydon cousins came to stay they had to keep the door shut, as passing a skeleton in a bowler hat, as they went to bed by candlelight, was not for the faint-hearted. Annie and Mary Jane simply said that the living were likely to cause them more trouble than poor old Boris. One moonlit night, some years later, when Bill had no further use for him, Lilian put Boris in a wheelbarrow, and took him across the village green and "down the moss," where she gave him a "decent burial." To date no one has reported the discovery of his remains.

Back in November, 1922, Lilian was enjoying her first term at the Secondary School. She won a competition for a scrapbook about the newly unearthed tomb of Tutankhamun, in the Valley of Kings in Egypt. Later, when the archaeologist Howard Carter visited the school, she was chosen to serve his tea!

Annie and Lilian at the gate of Rose House. Matt and Bel Ridley's cottage can be seen at the far side of the village hall.

The previous month had seen family rejoicing over good news from Blaydon when George Irving married his sister-in-law, Rachel (Ray). Ray had cared for his five children and made a home for them all for the past four years. In a letter to Annie, George described how Warwick, his eldest son, had cried when he told him of his intention to remarry, but when he realised that his Aunt Ray was to be the bride, he was happy. George and Ray had a further two children to complete their family — Harold, born in 1924, and Elizabeth, born in 1926.

By the mid-twenties, the chapel at Walton had replaced its harmonium with an organ that had to be pumped by hand whenever it was played. Matt Ridley took on the responsibility of the pumping and, whenever they could co-ordinate their spare time, Lilian taught herself to play the organ. She also taught in the Sunday school and, for some years, several of her younger cousins were members of her class.

At home, Mary Jane was becoming an ever more demanding responsibility. In the summer of 1925, while on holiday at the Height, she fell and broke her hip. She was now seventy-three and well beyond the average life-expectancy age of her time. The doctors decided to strap up the hip for what they were sure would be a relatively short time. As soon as he could, Billy brought her, complete with crutches, straight back to Annie. Mary Jane was not an easy patient. As she fought to regain her mobility and get herself "going again," it became obvious that she was lapsing mentally. She became obsessed with having to "walk to Castle Carrock" to start her "new job." Crutches, a broken hip, and arthritic knees were no impediment to this wily, determined woman. She took every opportunity to escape from Rose House. By the spring of 1926, she was an expert at sneaking out through the low back door and fleeing the village on her seemingly-jet-propelled crutches. She was always caught well before she reached the Lane End, but she became ever more devious in her bids for freedom.

When Lilian was at school, Annie was left alone to cope with the house, the shop, and Mary Jane. Getting her up and down stairs was the biggest problem. When Bill came home for the Easter break, he was shocked to see how care-worn Annie had become. He and Lilian took over the care of Mary Jane and the running of the house until the new term started. As soon as he got back to Newcastle, Bill wrote to Billy at the Height to ask for something to be done about the care of his grandmother. His mother, he said, had her living to earn, and he thought it was unfair to expect her to cope with Mary Jane as well.

Billy, the first one in the family to own a motor car, drove straight over to Walton and saw for himself the impossibility of what Annie was trying to do. He then went to see Bob and Edie at the Mill. He sat and talked to them in the kitchen for a long time without saying that there was anything amiss. When he got up to leave Bob walked back to the car with him. The car was a black soft-topped Riley and Billy always parked it at the top of the steep hill and walked down to the Mill. The car would not have been able to get back up the hill. In those early days of motoring, it was common in Cumberland to see passengers unloaded from cars to walk up the hills, often pushing the car as they climbed.

Bob was gone for some time. When he came back he simply said, "We're having mother." It had all been decided.

So Mary Jane returned to Walton Mill. Billy transported her in his car. He also arranged to take responsibility for taking her to Kate each Spring and to Lil in the Autumn. A horse and cart were still needed to get her up and down the hill.

Bob and Edie's daughter Edith was born on the 24th April, shortly after Mary Jane's arrival, a few days after the Duchess of York gave birth to Princess Elizabeth, and a few weeks before the General Strike that would bring such misery to the mining communities of Durham, Northumberland, West Cumberland and, more locally, to the miners of the Fell pits between Hallbankgate and Alston.

Although a very different woman, both mentally and physically, from the one who had marched out five years earlier, Mary Jane was still on the look-out for work that needed to be done. Within days of her arrival she noticed that the young woman hired to help in the house was having a tea-break. She immediately ordered her out into the yard to cut nettles.

Apart from such interesting incidents as having to rescue their hired help from nettle cutting, that kept them all on their toes, Edie coped well with Mary Jane and did her best to keep her happy. There were more people around to help when problems arose. Because of the three stone steps leading into the house, and a further four leading into the kitchen, Mary Jane didn't go missing.

She could never be idle. She polished Edie's silver-plated jugs so frequently and vigorously that there was no silver left. She spent her evenings darning and mending. She never used a thimble and when she affectionately rubbed her finger on Tom and Edna's faces they noticed its roughness, from a life-time of hard work and from so much pricking with a needle.

She didn't always recognise her grandchildren, often mistaking them for neighbours' children of bye-gone years, but she entertained them, as she had entertained Lilian, with tales of her own childhood. They all heard of how, as a small girl playing on the shore at Gretna, she and her friends went to investigate what they thought was a tree trunk washed up by the tide. It was a body.

Like all mothers of young children, Edie was a light sleeper and she knew when Mary Jane, who slept downstairs, in the back sitting room, was wandering in the night. Her mother-in-law was often back in the past in her night-time wanderings. Edie once found her sitting on a chair in the kitchen, in the middle of the night, with her bedroom lamp in front of her, driving a horse and cart to Gretna. To begin with they had placed the small lamp on the mantelpiece in her bedroom, but, even on crutches, she would manage to carry it around, take off the glass and turn up the flame. Afraid of them all being burned in their beds, Bob managed to fix the lamp to the ceiling.

John, who had returned to his childhood home a few years after his release from Dover Castle, was also living at the Mill at this time. He rented nearby fields and kept sheep until he had amassed sufficient capital to return South and farm independently at the Old Rectory Farm near Chingford. He gradually built up a dairy herd and ran a thriving milk business. He was the first person to sell milk in bottles in the Chingford area, guaranteeing delivery before 8.00 a.m. and enabling his customers to collect their milk from their doorsteps without having to come out to the milkman with a can.

Annie, at forty-eight, and no longer young herself, took a little while to recover from the stress of the previous months. The strain of the years of toil, particularly the nightly bread making, was beginning to tell. One Saturday afternoon, in June, a woman from the village came into the shop and begged to be allowed to buy one of the two loaves she could see at the back of the shop. Annie explained that they had been ordered by someone living outside the village who, unusually, hadn't yet collected them. At seven o'clock the village woman returned and, in tears, again begged to purchase one of the loaves. Annie relented. Two hours later, after the shop had been locked for the night, the customer who had ordered the bread originally, and who kept kennels, came to collect her two loaves. She was not pleased to be told that only one remained.

"You've really let me down Mrs Irving," she complained angrily, "now I've got nothing for the dogs' dinner."

"Dogs' dinner!" said Annie incredulously. "Have I been killing myself for a pack of dogs? There'll be no more bread sold here I can tell you."

Next day, at chapel, she told the congregation, and asked them to pass it on, that she would not be selling any more bread.

"We'll manage," she told Lilian. "It's only another year till Bill qualifies."

She had lost one customer but she had regained her life. There was also a sharp increase in the sale of flour. As long as she was careful, and she could never be anything else, they would be alright – and then came the news from Cargo.

In July, 1926, five-year-old Lily Edgar, playing outside in the sunshine, noticed the riot of summer flowers in a neighbour's garden. She walked up the garden path and picked a bunch of flowers before knocking at the door and presenting them happily to the lady of the house with the words, "Here you are. I've picked you a bunch of your pretty flowers."

Mary and Fred soon had a very irate neighbour on their doorstep.

The next day, Lily was suddenly taken ill. She died of pneumonia on the 18th July, and a light went out of all their lives. When Mary and Fred opened their door the following morning, their step, path and garden were strewn with flowers "for Lily" from the distraught neighbour who no longer wanted a single bloom in her own garden.

Two months later, Mary and Fred's son, George, aged twenty-three months, died on the 10th September. He had caught an infection that, like the illnesses that had killed the toddlers at Preston, began with a sore throat.

The following Spring, to compound it all, Mary gave birth to a full-term, still-born son. Annie was convinced that indescribable grief had contributed to this further terrible loss suffered by her sister. Their faith, as always, sustained them.

In Felling-on-Tyne, in 1927, work was well underway on George and Sally's new house. The dream was finally coming true, but there were hold-ups caused by the General Strike. They were having great difficulties getting the windows. The "new house, new baby" saying was also apt. With their sons now aged nineteen and fourteen, they hoped to be installed in the house before the new baby arrived in September.

The detached house had four bedrooms and a bathroom leading off a large landing upstairs. Downstairs there was a vestibule, hall, cloakroom and telephone room, a kitchen with a triplex grate and a walk-in pantry, a large drawing room and a dining room that could comfortably accommodate a sideboard, table and twelve magnificent dining chairs. There was a passage at the side of the kitchen for the removal of working boots and clothes. The wash house was in a separate building outside. Apart from the lounge, which had an electric fire, there was a gas fire in every room. Every time a room was re-decorated the gas fire surrounds were re-enamelled to match the decoration.

There was a monkey-puzzle tree in the garden, just like the one in the garden at Friarsgarth in Walton, after which the house was named. The dark brown hall floor was laid by Italian workmen who wouldn't let them see it until it was complete. It was finished just in time for their daughter Enid's birth. It had taken twenty-two years, but Sally got her house. It more than lived up to her expectations and the new baby crowned her delight. All the family, at different times, went to see and admire both the house and the baby girl who had come, somewhat unexpectedly, into their lives.

Every Friday morning, for many years, Sally went into Fenwicks in Newcastle and bought one item of willow-pattern Spode china to display in her house. She always had a coffee in Fenwicks, at the same time and at the same table every week. She shared the table with a woman that she had met on her first visit. They never met at any other time.

Annie's life in Rose House was somewhat different. Earlier in the year, in 1927, excitement was rising as Bill's Finals approached. Lilian was also studying hard for her School Certificate. Annie was anxious that she should have the opportunity to train for a career, perhaps in teaching, and asked her what she would like to do. Probably for the only time in her life, Lilian was less than truthful. A bit like Ruth with Naomi, she insisted that all she had ever dreamed of doing was working in the shop with her mother and helping her in the house and garden. She had been doing all the wall-papering since she was twelve and she enjoyed knitting, sewing, and gardening. She had a treadle-operated Singer sewing machine that had already more than paid for itself and, she said, she couldn't imagine anything better than the life they would be able to have together in the village with so many friends and family around them. To pacify Annie, she agreed to stay on into the sixth form and keep her options open. But her mind was made up.

"She'd done enough. I couldn't put her through it again," Lilian confessed years later. "She wasn't getting any younger and at least when Bill was away, she always had me around to help out. It all worked out right in the end."

Bill's results were expected in June and he had promised to send a telegram as soon as they were available. It was a nail-biting wait. Finally, on the 24th June, the news arrived. Annie, with Lilian on her heels, ran across the road to show her telegram to Mrs Bawden. Sending all the children out to play, Mrs Bawden immediately rang the school bell and brought all the village running to see what was amiss. When they heard the news, they all joined hands and began skipping and dancing on the green as they congratulated Annie.

All dressed up for the graduation.

Mrs Bawden wrote in the log book: "Received news today that William Irving who gained a minor scholarship from the school in 1915 had gained his MD at Armstrong's College, Newcastle with Honours. He was first on the list and won the Philipson scholarship valued at £58 per annum. School was dismissed at 3.00 p.m. and the children with great gusto raised their school flag in honour of their old pupil."

Dr William Irving (aged 22), 1927.

Annie raided her Post Office Savings Account to dress herself, Lilian and, of course, Bill, in new outfits for his graduation. The event was commemorated with photographs. Nothing that had happened before, or would happen later, could ever compare with how she felt this day. This was her moment.

8

RABBITS AND RHUBARB

Bill worked at the Royal Victoria Infirmary in Newcastle, first as House Physician to Dr Horsley Drummond, and then as House Surgeon to Professor Grey Turner, before becoming a locum for a General Practice, run by a Dr Goodman, at Seaham Harbour, on the North East coast. He was particularly interested in the treatment of cancer, the disease that had killed his father, and in which he would eventually specialise. Surgery would always be his passion.

One of his first purchases, now that he was beginning to earn a little money, was a 1926 SD Triumph motor bike that enabled him to travel quickly between Newcastle and Walton whenever he had time off. On one of his visits he brought them a wireless, an invention that they had heard about but never seen. News of its presence in the parlour at Rose House spread quickly. Most of the customers coming into the shop wanted to see and listen to this marvel of the modern age. Kate's daughter, Muriel, was a regular visitor to Rose House and she remembered listening to Children's Hour for the first time and being startled by the voice coming out of the gigantic horn on the table. Care had to be taken not to spill the acid and the large heavy battery had to be transported into Brampton whenever it needed re-charging. Fortunately, there was now an occasional bus service to and from the village.

Muriel came to Rose House whenever a pig was to be killed at Swainsteads. She couldn't bear to listen to its tormented squeals. Although pig-stickers were a thing of the past there was still a distinct lack of humanity in the more modern method, where the pig was held down on a butching stool and had its throat stuck or slit with a gully. The noise was blood-curdling.

In 1928, women were given the right to vote at the age of twenty-one and the first step towards equality with men was finally climbed. There was still a long way to go, but Annie was happy with her lot in Walton. She was independent and the shop was more than able to support two of them in the way they wanted to live. Life in the village revolved around the school, the shop, the Church, the Chapel and the village hall which was only a few yards away from Rose House. The village hall provided activities and entertainment for the whole community. It hosted dances, social evenings and occasional film shows, as well as Sunday school parties, Sales of Work, and Jumble Sales. Annie was now involved in the organisation of many of these events. The Women's Institute and the Mother's Union held their weekly meetings in the hall. Annie, Kate and Edie were all members of both of these organisations. There were regular bus trips from the village to places of interest and to the seaside at Silloth.

Walton Women's Institute in the 1930s.
Annie (left) and Kate (right) are in the middle of the front row.

In May, 1928, £1 and 10s notes were introduced, adding to the existing large white £5 notes. They were a mixed blessing in the village shop, where shopping bills rarely reached £1 and were mostly under 10s. It became necessary to carry an even larger float of change. All the money was kept in a drawer in the counter, with compartments for different coins and notes, before being transferred to the greater security of a lockable desk top that stood behind a screen on the right hand side of the counter. Annie quickly learned to leave any note offered in payment on the counter until the customer was satisfied with the change given. She had a similar system with half-crowns and florins.

As soon as Lilian left school and began working full time in the shop, Annie was concerned that there should be no repetition of her own situation at the Mill. Lilian, she insisted, must have some money that was in her own name, and half-a-crown was duly deposited in Lilian's Post Office account every week.

Ill health had forced Mrs Bawden's retirement from the village school in April, 1929. Another era had ended. She was sadly missed in the village and in Rose House in particular.

Things were also changing in the lives of Annie's extended family. Mary and Fred moved to Carlisle where they took out a mortgage to help them to buy 6 Clift Street, a small terraced house near the Infirmary, for £330. The near loss of their remaining child, Bill, had hastened their move from their cottage in Cargo, where Fred worked on a farm. Like his younger brother, George, Bill Edgar was struck down with an illness, probably meningitis, from which he was not expected to recover. He had been unconscious for two days when the doctor told them that there was no hope of his survival. Promising to return soon, he left his box on the bed while he made another call.

While he was absent, a couple from the chapel called to see Mary and found her sitting by the bedside of her dying child. In less than an hour after they left, Mary noticed the little boy stirring. He reached out his arm to touch the doctor's box. On his return the doctor was amazed to find him awake. When Mary recounted the story of the miracle to her chapel friends they asked her what time the recovery had started.

"That was when we were all praying for him in the chapel," they told her. For the rest of her life, Mary never doubted the power of prayer.

Fred thought that the damp in their cottage may have caused the children's illnesses and they made up their minds to move. Fred went to work as a guard on the railway. The house at Clift Street, easily accessible by bus, became a haven for anyone in the family with a hospital appointment. They always went to visit Mary first. She knew her way round the Infirmary and went with the patients to make sure that they found the right department for their problem. She always took them home with her for refreshment and conversation. Hospital visits became real social events.

In Felling-on-Tyne, George and Sally's eldest son, Archie, now twenty-one, joined the Merchant Navy and set sail on his first voyage across the Atlantic in "The Glasgow." The ship's engines blew up half way across the ocean. Sally first heard of the disaster when she saw a newspaper placard while out shopping. Full details of the event and its resulting casualties were slow to reach the families back home. Sally walked into the newspaper offices at Newcastle every day, pushing Enid in the pram, so that she could talk to the congregating reporters and try to find out what had happened to her son. The news, when it came, was good. The News Chronicle reporter who discovered that Archie was unharmed actually lodged with the people next door.

John, in Chingford, the last of Annie's siblings to marry, surprised them all when he announced his marriage to Ella in March, 1930. Ella was forty and John was forty-four. Their only child, Jim, was born the next year. The new house in Clift Street had also produced a new baby. Mary and Fred's son, Raymond, was born in June, 1930, amid much family rejoicing, and a crashing global economy.

By August, the month that the Duchess of York gave birth to Princess Margaret, unemployment in the country had reached two million. It would go on climbing. The stock market crash that led to the depression and the "threadbare thirties" brought misery to members of all levels of society but was felt most among the out-of-work poor. The depths of the poverty would be beyond the imagination of later generations. Living conditions in many of the towns were appalling. Country people once again fared a little better. They grew their own vegetables, gathered the fruits of the hedgerows – particularly brambles and crab apples – and were grateful for the abundance of the rabbits, first introduced by the Romans, in the fields and on the fells. Gamekeepers on the country estates were fully occupied trying to catch the many hungry poachers who roamed the woods at night.

In the village shop at Walton Annie and Lilian continued to earn enough to support them. They had their hens in the back yard and they made full use of their small garden. The stone shelves in the pantry were always well stocked with jams and bottled fruits. A bucket of pickled eggs stood in the corner. They knew where to gather the best brambles and never missed out on the mushroom season. Annie gathered mushrooms every September, as she had done in her childhood, for as long as she lived in

Walton. She was always an early riser and would be back in the village, with her laden basket, before most of the inhabitants were up and about.

Some of the people in the village, who had fruit trees in their gardens, kept her supplied with damsons, plums, pears and apples that she then re-sold. One local man had been supplying her with luscious rhubarb for years. Annie and Lilian, however, always used their own inferior product. They couldn't understand how he managed to produce such large, juicy sticks of rhubarb that were sold almost as soon as they were displayed. Lilian, with her love of gardening, read all the books available to try to discover what she must do to produce a comparable crop. For years she and Annie asked the supplier for his secret. Eventually he relented under their combined pressure and said that he would tell them if they solemnly promised never to reveal his secret. They agreed.

"It's easy," he told them, "I just empty the netty bucket round the rhubarb every few weeks."

As they looked at him, aghast, he said anxiously, "Now you did promise you wouldn't tell anybody."

He needn't have worried. They never told a soul. The quality of the rhubarb grown at Rose House didn't improve either.

Bill now had a 1929, 250cc, Rudge Whitworth motor bike with more room for his pillion passenger. He was accompanied on most of his visits to Walton by Eva Anderson, a staff nurse from the Royal Victoria Infirmary, who was always known as "Andy." She had grown up in South Shields where her father, John Anderson, was a shipping butcher. Andy was the middle one of his five daughters.

Bill and Andy were married at South Shields on 21st April, 1931. Annie and Lilian travelled there by train and spent the weekend with Andy's family. They were joined at the ceremony by their Blaydon relatives, including Abe and Lizzie, George and Ray, and Polly and Essie. Essie's father, yet another William Irving, had died when she was fourteen. She and George's daughter, Mary, had been the most frequent Blaydon visitors to Walton over the years. They were nearest in age to Lilian and neither of them ever lost touch with her. Their letters ensured that everybody was always up to date with the latest family news.

George and Sally Wilkinson, accompanied by Enid, also attended the wedding. Bill had visited them regularly while he was based in Newcastle and, on hearing of the wedding, their son, Walton, commented laughingly, "He was always complaining about the nurses at the hospital and then he went and married one of them."

George and Sally were keen to hear if all was well with Edie at the Mill. Another baby was expected there in May. They heard how five-year-old Edith had now joined Tom and Edna at the village school and was causing them problems at dinner times. She couldn't run fast enough to get them back to school in time for the start of the afternoon session. As they didn't like staying in school over the dinner break, Annie had solved the problem by suggesting that they bring their sandwiches to Rose House every day. This happy arrangement carried on until well after the new baby, Margaret, started school.

Bill and Andy spent their honeymoon in Conwy, North Wales. They bought Annie and Lilian a pair of small silver-coloured salt and pepper pots with "Conwy" on the sides. No other holiday memento can have been better used. The salt and pepper pots

Bill and Andy leaving for Conwy.

were in daily use until the dawn of the new millennium. The young couple made their first home at Stephenson Road in Newcastle and Andy continued nursing while Bill travelled daily to Seaham Harbour. Towards the end of the year he secured a permanent position in a practice in West Hartlepool, with a Dr English, and their letters for Lilian's 21st birthday in November were full of this forthcoming move.

"We're getting very thrilled about West Hartlepool," Bill wrote. "We've got a house, 'Stanley House,' Grange Road. The rent is fifteen shillings per week plus rates. It will be a little less than here. It's a very nice house. The kitchen has nice cupboards and drawers, a big larder and a plate rack. We have six rooms and three attics.

"It's more than we want or can furnish but will last us for years. It's very convenient – just a few doors past Dr English's house. The owner was the last tenant and he has left the place very clean. The painting and papers are all decent. They've also left a good bit of lino on the hall and kitchen. So really we're very lucky. It has gas for lighting which is pretty awful but we'll soon get used to it. Dr English said he would see whether they would install electricity for us. He was very nice when we saw him yesterday. We also met his sister. She was very charming and gave us tea. Dr English said he would take the house for us if necessary from today, but he would stand the expense until we came. Wasn't that nice of him? He said it's only about £4 or £5, neither here nor there. We thought after how nice to be him, but it was very decent of him. Goodman would have made us take it for the sake of the job.

"I'm having some men tomorrow to estimate the removal. I think it best to have two or three, then you can compare. We'll be nicely moved for Christmas."

They had sent Lilian a gold watch and an evening bag for her birthday. She had several other presents and cards. All her birthday cards, in the fashion of the day, were brightly coloured postcards which cost 1d to post. Significantly, everything was posted on the 19th November and nothing was late for her birthday next day. One of the cards was from Millie Gray, of "The Grove," the far cottage in the row in front of Rose House, who was a regular customer in the shop. She purchased the card from Annie and posted it in the village. It was the first time that they had received anything with a Walton postmark. Lilian was delighted. Annie reflected, almost unbelievingly, on the difference between their situation now and what it had been at Lilian's birth.

Earlier that year, Annie had lost an old friend. Bel Ridley, who had first befriended her when she was a frightened girl at the Mill, died suddenly and without warning. Because their landlord wanted their cottage, she and Matt were about to move to one of the Wilson Homes in the village. The Wilson Homes had been built by a local philanthropist, but Bel, now 87, didn't want to leave her present home beside the chapel.

Matt had been to the bus stop to meet their daughter who was paying her weekly visit. As they passed the school on their way home they saw Bel shaking a table cloth outside and waved to her. When they went into the cottage a few minutes later they found her lying on the floor. They ran for Annie but Bel never regained consciousness. She had suffered a massive stroke. Annie, as she did with so many of her neighbours, performed the final service for her friend and laid her out in the tiny bedroom.

Matt and Bel Ridley on their Golden Wedding Day.

It didn't seem long since all the members of the chapel had been celebrating the old couple's golden wedding and had made a bouquet of flowers for Bel to hold in the photograph taken on their special day. Matt had to move to the Wilson Homes alone, but he was grateful that she had been spared the trauma of such an upheaval. As always, the people of the village rallied round to support him as, in the past, he and Bel had supported so many of them.

George V made his first Christmas day broadcast in December and started a new royal tradition. The best china came out of the Press and Annie served tea and a generous slice of Christmas cake to all the friends and family gathered round the wireless in the parlour. Christmas was always her favourite season and their hopes were bright for the New Year.

Joy and sadness, however, always came in equal measure. They were soon to be stunned by the receipt of tragic news. On 10th January, 1932, George and Sally's daughter, Enid, aged four, died of pneumonia. She was the sixth of Mary Jane's grandchildren to die in early childhood. During her short life, Enid had suffered a lot from chest infections. Sally, an expert needle-woman, had done her best to protect her daughter from cold. When she sent all Enid's clothes to the Mill for the new baby, Margaret, they discovered that every beautiful little hand made dress was lined with flannel.

In the summer of 1932 Annie had a letter from West Hartlepool to say that Andy was expecting a baby in January of the next year. It was her second pregnancy. She had already suffered one miscarriage. Mary, in Carlisle, was also expecting a baby in January, at the age of forty-four. Annie fretted about them both. All went well. Her first grandchild, to her delight named Robert after his grandfather, arrived safely, as did Mary's daughter, another Margaret. Bill had now swapped his motor bike for a car, and they brought Robert to Walton to introduce him to some of his relatives as soon as Andy was able to travel. It was a journey he would make many times. Lilian put a chair on the village green and photographed Annie and Robert with her Box Brownie camera.

Mary Jane had had a grandchild and a great grandchild in the same month. She was now seventy-nine and still suffering agonies with her hip. It was six years since the doctors had strapped it up. Her eyesight was failing. She had developed cataracts and could no longer see to read the paper or to sew. Edna remembered seeing her rubbing her arthritic knees with methylated spirits crying, "Oh, my poor knees, my poor knees."

Edie spent time reading aloud to her out of the Cumberland News and tried to pick out stories that might be of interest. The hatches, matches and despatches would, of course, be the first columns to be scanned. It was always cheering for Mary Jane to hear of so many younger people that she had "seen away."

9

FIRE AT THE MILL

Later in 1933, Lil and Dick left Ghyll Head, at Wigton, and moved to a farm at Steeple Aston near Oxford, where, as so often happened with a new house, they were soon looking forward to a new addition to their family.

Billy took Mary Jane to Kate at Swainsteads for her Spring holiday on the first weekend in February, 1934. She was taken ill almost immediately. Annie went straight away to stay with Kate to help with the round-the-clock nursing of their mother. Eight-year-old Muriel was despatched to Rose House to stay with Lilian and go to school from there. Pneumonia set in and Mary Jane slipped quietly away during the early hours of Friday, 9th February. She was eighty years old. Jim and his wife, "Preston Annie," and John came to stay at Rose House until after the funeral.

Mary Jane was well known in the locality and they knew it would be a well-attended funeral. Ned, in Canada, and Lil at Oxford, expecting her third child, were the only two of her ten children unable to attend. Lil's son, William, was Mary Jane's youngest grandchild and the only one to be born after her death.

It was customary for people attending funerals to be given a sit down, knife and fork, funeral tea afterwards and it was a matter of some importance that a good spread should be provided. Hams were boiled. Bread, fruit loaves, sponge cakes, plate cakes, gingerbread, rock buns and scones were baked in vast quantities. Tomatoes were bought and eggs hard boiled to fill bowls on the table. Pickles, chutneys, jam, butter and cream were also provided, along with freshly mixed containers of Colman's mustard. Annie contributed ingredients for the baking from the shop and farm produce from Swainsteads was supplemented by contributions from the Height and from the Mill. There would have to be several sittings at the large table in the dining room. As Mary Jane had been laid out in the sitting room, Kate and Annie got men from the farm to come and move furniture so that they could transform a bedroom into a sitting room for their visitors to use while waiting for their meal.

Time had to be allowed on the Saturday for the whole family to go into Carlisle to buy the obligatory new black outfits, including hats and coats, so that Mary Jane, for whom respectability had always been everything, would not be let down by their appearance. Lilian had a black chiffon dress with oval inserts on the sleeves and bodice in a yellow material. At a later date she replaced the yellow with a soft pink material that better suited her pale complexion.

On Sunday, all the family took their children to Swainsteads to pay their last respects to Mary Jane. Most of them accepted this ritual as normal, but Billy's son, twelve-year-old Jardine, found the whole experience traumatic and howled loudly as Billy propelled him, unwillingly, into the room.

While her daughters were dealing with the catering practicalities, Mary Jane's sons, with the help of Watsons, the Brampton undertakers, were finalising the details of the funeral itself. Very few of the large number of mourners had transport and so it was decided that everyone would walk the three-quarters of a mile to the churchyard for the 2 o'clock service. Five of her six sons, Jim and George, Billy and John, and Bob with Kate's husband, Peter, carried her coffin through the village, led by the undertaker and followed by the long procession of mourners. The service, in the custom of the day, was conducted around the graveside.

And so the farm labourer's daughter from Gretna, whose own life had been one of unceasing labour, finally rested, with her second husband, the jovial miller, in Walton churchyard. Like so many of her generation, her descendants are now scattered around the globe, like the proverbial seeds on the wind, or grains of sand from the desert. It would be hard to find an occupation, trade or profession that has not been represented by one of them. Most of them, at some time, have listened with admiration and amusement to stories of the legend that was Mary Jane.

After the funeral came the sorting out of the small bequests in her will, made some years previously, and the final settlement of Annie's grandfather Edward Blenkinsop's will, made in 1880. Annie was given power to act for Ned, in Canada. The properties in Castle Carrock were sold, for a pittance, because of the depression, and the money transferred to Ned. A few years later he inherited another detached property in Castle Carrock, which also had to be sold at a time when there was no money around for such transactions. It fetched the magnificent sum of £200.

Annie felt that, once again, her eldest brother had been denied the full benefit of his inheritance. It was around this time that she developed her aversion to wills. She was adamant that nothing would ever persuade her to make a will. True to her character, she never changed her mind and, as luck would have it, it didn't really matter. She frequently recalled the will of "old Uncle Isaac" who had left all his money to Mary Jane and the three Blenkinsop children with the proviso that £5 a year be paid to Mary Jane's sister-in-law for life. Unfortunately, by the time of his death, the amount that he left was so small that the £5 a year became a terrible drain on the family finances.

Another uncle had generously made a will leaving all his money for the education and maintenance of Ned, Jim and Annie, but had managed to spend it all in the Castle Carrock pubs well before his death.

"Wills," Annie proclaimed, "cause nothing but trouble for the poor folk left to clear up the mess." Her family might not have agreed with her, but they knew better than to argue the point.

In October 1934, Bill who was now partner to Dr English in the Medical Practice, began a long association with the Hartlepool Hospitals when he became an honorary assistant surgeon. He would become Honorary Surgeon in 1942.

Lilian met her future husband, Nicholas Killeen, shortly before her grandmother's death. Nick was hired on a farm outside the village and came regularly into the village shop. Like Lilian, he also attended the dances in the village halls in Walton and the surrounding area. As his surname suggested, Nick was of Irish descent. All four of his grandparents had come to Cleator Moor (Little Ireland) on the West Cumbrian coast during the years of the Irish potato famine. His paternal grandfather was a cooper and his maternal grandmother (Granny Kennedy) had a fruit and vegetable barrow on Whitehaven market.

His father, Peter, had run away to sea as a young man and told hair-raising tales about life on the ocean wave. He was once trapped in a cabin when the ship was on fire and, although he escaped, he suffered nightmares for the rest of his life. He frequently terrified the family in the night with cries of, "Fire! Fire!"

After the fire-at-sea experience, Peter went into the Whitehaven pits. He was a widower with two small children when he married Martha Starkey, a widow with four children, whose first husband had been killed in a mining disaster. Nick was the only child of the second marriage. After spending some time in the North East, the family moved to a small cottage at High Fell near Hallbankgate. Nick was eight years old when he and his family arrived at Brampton Junction. They walked to High Fell from the station carrying all their possessions, which included one piece of furniture – a kitchen table. His love of the Cumbrian fells and countryside began on that day.

High Fell.

As he walked through the lanes to their new home and compared it with the streets of Newcastle he thought that he had come to fairyland. His father, Peter, and older brother, David Starkey, went to work in the fell pits. Davy was a highly intelligent, self-educated young man who became an expert on border history. Like Nick, he loved the fells and the countryside.

It was an unspeakable tragedy that he had to spend so much of his life digging for coal, underground, in wet, eighteen-inch seams. Nick had desperately wanted to be a joiner but there was no money to buy the tools that he needed for his apprenticeship.

He became a farmer's boy, working first at High Fell farm for Ridley Evans. He then went to work on a farm in the Penrith area. It was a terrible mistake. The conditions would have been considered harsh a hundred years earlier.

It was a large farm and all the hired men had to sleep on straw mattresses in a room above an outhouse. Every night before they went to bed they had to beat the mattresses with sticks and chase out all the rats. When, at the end of his contract, he told the farmer that he was leaving, the man refused to give him a lift to the station with the tin trunk that held all his belongings. A kind-hearted postman took pity on the small, struggling, fifteen-year-old and wheeled the trunk to the station for him on his bike. He worked on farms closer to home after this experience.

Although life was not easy on the farm near Walton, it was better than many. He learned to be philosophical about the food provided. The farmer's wife at this farm allowed one of the farm cats to sit on the table while she was baking and stroked it frequently with pastry covered fingers. Scones, rock buns and plate cakes were always liberally filled with cat hairs.

Like Lilian, Nick had been brought up in a non-conformist, strictly tee-total household. His father, Peter, had been converted from Roman Catholicism by a street preacher in Newcastle. One of Nick's earliest memories of life at High Fell was of seeing the Catholic priest from Warwick Bridge, in flowing robes, striding through the fields to round up the straying member of his church. Nick sat on the stairs and listened in absolute terror to the verbal tirade unleashed against his father by the man of God. The priest threatened excommunication and promised the family's certain destruction in the flames of Hell. Nick then watched in shocked admiration as Peter snatched the priest's stick, which had been raised to strike him, and chased its owner, who had to gather up his skirts to run, down the steep hill to the stone stile into the field. As the priest cleared the stile, Peter snapped the stick in half and hurled it over the wall to its fleeing owner. Annie was very impressed when she heard this story. She was sure that she would get on well with Peter and Martha.

Most of the property in the Hallbankgate and Lanercost areas was owned by Lady Cecelia, daughter of the ninth Earl of Carlisle and the much loved Lady Rosalind. Lady Cecelia was married to barrister Charles Roberts who, during his time as an M.P., had served as a government minister. The Roberts family belonged to the Liberal Party and were highly respected in the area. They lived at Boothby mansion house near Lanercost.

Annie and Lilian were strong supporters of the Liberals. In the election of 1935, when the Liberal candidate was Wilfred Roberts, son of Charles and Lady Cecelia, Annie held the Walton Committee rooms at Rose House. Lilian went with other supporters to a large house at the top of Station Road in Brampton to address envelopes for the campaign. This was another loyalty that she shared with Nick. Nick and Davy loathed the opposing Conservative Party with a bitterness that would be life-long. In earlier years they had seen Peter and Martha suffer the indignity of the Means Test. Even in old age Nick was heard to fume that he "could smell a Tory" when he met one. Wilfred Roberts was duly elected, as M.P. for North Cumberland, in the 1935 election amid great local rejoicing. Edna, from the Mill, happened to be in Brampton to witness some of the celebrations. She saw the jubilant crowd thrusting the newly elected M.P. on to scrap man Dick McGee's cart and heard calls of, "Let's put t'od feller on as well."

Charles was unceremoniously hoisted up beside his son. The grandson and son-in-law of the ninth Earl were hauled triumphantly and incongruously around the market place in a commandeered cart that normally carried much humbler loads.

In Jarrow, in the North East, two thirds of the male inhabitants were out of work following the closure of Palmers shipyard. It had been a brutal place to work but was infinitely better than no work at all. The people of Jarrow elected "Red" Ellen Wilkinson as their M.P.

For Mary's sons, five-year-old Ray and his older brother Bill, 1935 was remembered for an event of far more interest than the election. Annie travelled into Carlisle to collect them from Clift Street and take them to the Lonsdale cinema to see the film Pinnochio. They went for tea afterwards in a nearby café.

Annie's special relationship with her sister Mary was a lifelong commitment. She never went empty handed to visit and Mary's family always remembered the new shoes that Annie made it her duty to provide every Easter throughout their school lives. Annie herself had spent her childhood with her feet squashed into crippling shoes that always seemed to be far too small. She blamed the painful bunions that afflicted her throughout her adult life on the fact that she had never possessed a well-fitting pair of shoes when she was young.

Davy was now working at Midgeholme colliery near Alston, where the seams of coal were deeper and, although not well paid, was earning more than Nick. All the fell pits were drift mines and the men walked, not always upright, to the coal face, often a long way from the surface. As he and Lilian were saving for their marriage, Nick joined Davy at Midgeholme and began his underground work as a putter, pushing the tubs of coal up the steep roadway to the pit bank. They cycled the five miles up the fell road from High Fell to Midgeholme every day, in all weathers. The homeward journeys, when their shifts were over, were downhill all the way.

Nick plucked up the courage to arrange an interview with Lady Cecelia to ask if he and Lilian might be able to rent one of her houses. He was graciously received and asked to sit down. The interview was long, thorough and pleasant. At the end came the crunch question: "Now tell me, Mr Killeen – your young lady – is she in the family way?"

She beamed as he stuttered his denial and then said, "Well we can afford to wait for a good house then, can't we? Don't worry, I'll make sure you get one."

They had to wait three years, but she kept her promise.

January, 1936, was a bitterly cold month. In the early hours of Monday 20th January, Annie and Lilian heard a terrible commotion outside. They looked out to see the men of the village slipping and sliding along the road as they rushed past Rose House. Annie flung open the window to ask what was happening.

"The Mill's on fire!" she was told. They then saw the fire-engine from Brampton racing past. They knew that there was nothing they could do but they had a terrible night and were very relieved when a man returning to the village told them that no one was hurt. Early in the morning, they switched on the wireless as they were having a quick cup of tea before going to the Mill, and they heard the news that George V had died at Sandringham during the night. He would be succeeded by his eldest son, Edward, Prince of Wales. There was, as yet, no hint of the impending crisis. When they got to the Mill they found that the house had been saved by the wind having changed direction just as the flames from the fire, which had started in the adjoining barn, were reaching the building. Local people had worked alongside the firemen to put out the blaze, using buckets of water from the millpond.

Bob had spotted the fire from the bedroom window at 1.00 a.m. The hired man had run into Walton to the telephone, shouting for help as he ran through the village. The Mill family were quickly dressed and evacuated. Tom was suffering from 'flu' and their neighbours from across the river put him and his two younger sisters to bed in their cottage.

Edna described how the flames were going up into the sky as they rushed to get the cows out of the byre under the barn before taking them up to Hillhead farm for shelter. The byre roof fell in just after they got the cows safely outside. Annie looked with horror at the devastation around her, but, like the family at the Mill, was thankful that no lives had been lost. The cause of the fire was never established but one theory was that a passing tramp might have been smoking while sheltering in the barn. Everything was rebuilt in the summer.

Bill and Andy had now moved from Grange Road to Granville Avenue in West Hartlepool. Annie's second grandson, named William after his father and known as "Billy," arrived on the 21st of August. Visits to Walton were now very lively occasions.

November, 1936, saw the arrival in London of the Jarrow marchers. Their plight touched the nation, but they arrived back home to find that their unemployment benefit had been cut because they had made themselves unavailable for the non-existent work. The abdication of Edward VIII the next month was, in Annie's opinion, "good riddance to bad rubbish." Although she always sympathised with the poor royal family, who never seemed to have much say in who they were going to marry, there were limits to the behaviour that could be tolerated. She and Lilian listened scornfully to the abdication speech on their wireless, now a more modern appliance, without a horn, that stood on a small table to the left of the parlour fireplace. Duty and responsibility came high on Annie's list of priorities. George VI and his family were much more to her liking and the coronation, in May 1937, was celebrated wholeheartedly, even though there were few commemorative objects available. It was the third coronation of Annie's lifetime and she read the newspaper accounts avidly, comparing the coverage with that given to George V in 1911 and to Edward VII in 1902.

Later that year, Annie's brother Jim and "Preston Annie" arrived as usual to spend their summer holidays at Rose House. They were accompanied, this time, by a neurotic Siamese cat called Bonzo. Bonzo's favourite pastime when upset, and he was upset easily and often, was to viciously scratch the legs of the nearest person. Annie, Lilian, and any customers who crossed his path were terrified of him. Annie instructed his fond owners that he must be kept in their bedroom as much as possible. One morning, as she was trying to do her washing, Bonzo ran downstairs and escaped through the back door. Preston Annie accused her of letting him out on purpose.

"You're welcome here any time," Annie told Jim, once Bonzo had been recaptured, "but that cat isn't. He'll lose me all my trade. You'll have to find somewhere else to stay while you've got him."

Jim went to see Kate at Swainsteads and the holidaymakers moved lodgings. Bonzo terrified his new hosts as well. The fish for his tea had been left on the doorstep while they settled him into his new surroundings. Jim went to collect the fish just as the farm cats were finishing an unexpectedly tasty meal. Everybody was very relieved when Bonzo went back to Preston.

Jim died very suddenly early the next year. He was sixty-two. It was a great shock. Preston Annie had a sister who was housekeeper to Lord Londonderry in Ireland. She accepted an invitation to travel to Ireland, with Bonzo, to spend some time getting over her bereavement, and they were duly settled into the housekeeper's quarters.

Unfortunately, Bonzo looked out of the window and saw the grooms exercising the horses. He went berserk and attacked Preston Annie, lacerating her legs. Her sister was horrified. She went to find a footman and a gun. That was the end of Bonzo.

10

TAKING THE GOAT BY THE HORNS

Annie celebrated her sixtieth birthday in April, 1938, shortly after her brother Jim's death. Lilian and Bill began pressurising her to plan to give up the shop when Lilian married. To help persuade her, Bill explained that if he made her a regular allowance he would be able to set it against his income tax.

Afternoon tea at Rose House.

The work involved in running Rose House, still without either electricity or water, was more than enough at this stage in her life. It was time, they told her, to retire.

Nick and Lilian got the key to their first house in June. It was one of a group of five cottages at High Bow Bank, fifty yards over the hill from Low Bow Bank. It was reached by a long unmade-up lonning from Kirkhouse. The High Road between Castle Carrock and Hallbankgate ran along the top of the fields that rose up behind the nearby beech woods. Annie knew it well.

Kirkhouse farm at the bottom of the lonning had once been owned by one of her Blenkinsop uncles and she had played in the area during her early childhood. There was a brickworks beside the farm. Farlam Parish Church was up the steep Shop Hill that led from Kirkhouse to Farlam lane end and the bus stop on the main Carlisle to Alston road. There was a regular bus service through Brampton to Carlisle. The farm and the warm brickworks were a magnet for the many tramps who roamed the area seeking shelter for the winter nights. Shop Hill was so called because of the mine-owners' shop that had once stood at the top, opposite the Church. In earlier times the miners in the fell pits had been paid in tokens that could only be cashed at this shop.

As soon as they had their key, Nick and Lilian got out their tandem, which they kept at Rose House, and cycled off to view their house. Cycling was one of the most popular leisure pursuits of the thirties and they had travelled many miles on the tandem in their spare time, going, on one occasion, as far as Hartlepool to visit Bill and Andy. As though cycling to work, pushing tubs of coal, and touring the area on the tandem were not enough to keep him fit, Nick was also a fell runner.

June was an ideal month to see High Bow Bank for the first time. As they pushed the tandem over the top of the lonning they saw their whitewashed stone house about fifty yards in front of them. There was a row of three houses set at a right angle down the right hand side of the area. Another detached house was to the left of their house, beside the field gate and the path that was a short cut to Hallbankgate and High Fell. The gardens for two of the row-of-three houses were on the left of the road at the hill top and the green-leafed beech trees, a group of which were known to the Bow Bank children as the "Bluebell Wood", stood protectively behind the gardens. Forty years later, Nick and Lilian revisited High Bow Bank and were devastated by its new closed-in appearance, but now it was a vibrant community, idyllically situated.

The front door of their house opened straight into the large living kitchen with a partitioned area just inside the door that served as a cloakroom. The black-leaded grate was on the left-hand wall. There was a window looking out to the front of the house and another looking onto the long back cottage garden, ablaze with flowers. The door to the staircase, leading to two double bedrooms, was on the right-hand wall beside the doors to the large scullery, outhouse and back door. There was a walk-in pantry leading off the back wall of the kitchen. The scullery had been partitioned off to provide a bathroom, which held a new, white-enamelled bath and a wall-mounted electric water heater. There was a large white sink and wooden draining board in the scullery, with a cold water tap above the sink. Lilian was ecstatic.

High Bow Bank.

There was a gate at the left-hand side of the house that led onto a path past a rose garden before joining the main garden. A large white climbing rose was in full bloom up the side of the house. The fact that there was no sewerage was irrelevant. They had electricity and they had an indoor water supply. The rent was 3/6d per week.

Annie and Lilian went to High Bow Bank by bus on the Saturday morning so that Annie could see the house and help with the measuring up for new wallpaper, lino and curtains. Nick walked down from High Fell, with Martha and Peter, and other members of his family, to meet them there. Annie said that it would be a shame to miss the opportunity of having so many workers on site, so they all set about stripping off the old wallpaper in the kitchen and bedrooms.

The wedding was to be two months later, on the 20th August, which they thought would give them plenty of time to get everything ready. Nick painted all the ceilings and the walls of the scullery and outhouse. He also re-whitewashed the outside walls. Lilian did all the papering and re-painted the internal woodwork, which was a depressing dark brown colour, in pale cream. It took several coats. Annie insisted that she could manage the shop by herself for a week so that Lilian could cycle the seven miles over to High Bow Bank and concentrate on the decorating.

They bought the rolls of new lino in Brampton and transported them to Farlam lane end on the bus. While Lilian was busying herself making the curtains, Nick was building a new lean-to shed for coal and gardening tools. Because of the general state of the economy, they were able to buy good, solid furniture in the Carlisle sale rooms for very little money. They bought a large mirrored sideboard, with ornately carved doors, an extending polished table, and four leather dining chairs for £5. A further £5 bought two black leather armchairs and a matching couch. A large chest of drawers and a bedstead for the spare bedroom cost another £5.

They bought a new utility bedroom suite for the larger bedroom. The window had to be taken out to get the wardrobe into the room, as the stairs were too narrow and awkward. Lilian scattered the floors with mats that she had made over the last few years. The largest mat was in front of the new brass fender around the grate. Nick fitted shelves around the sink and draining board which they concealed with a curtain.

Annie, who said that they would need a good store cupboard to see them through the winter months if they should be snowed-in, stocked the pantry as part of her wedding present.

The running down of stock in the shop now began in earnest and customers were told of the intention to stop trading. As she surveyed the sheer quantity, range and variety of goods that had to be disposed of, Annie reflected, almost unbelievingly, that it had all started with a jar of sweets. She, of course, kept a good supply of the non-perishable items, including tins of salmon, meat and fruit, for her own use, stored in her pantry. The bus service to Brampton made it easier for people to shop outside the village, but Annie didn't want to leave her loyal customers without a more convenient alternative. She told a Brampton grocer and a butcher of her intention to close her shop so that they could take the opportunity to build up delivery rounds to the village. She made lists of the names and addresses of people who would like them to call. Neither of them ever forgot how she had helped them with this information.

Lilian, ever practical, chose a navy blue suit and hat for her wedding outfit. She insisted that Annie must be the person who would give her away. To avoid upsetting any of her eleven female cousins she asked Nick's sister, Mary Starkey, to be her bridesmaid. Mary worked in Jacksons' draper's shop in Brampton. Davy was best man.

On the morning of the wedding, which was to be a small family occasion, the bride got up early to scrub the stone slabs of the shop floor before covering the counter and the parlour table with white tablecloths for the food for the reception. They borrowed chairs from the village hall to help with the seating. The car, that had been hired to transport Nick and his family from High Fell, also took Annie and Lilian the short distance from Rose House to the chapel for the 11 o'clock service. The families from the Mill, Swainsteads, High Fell and Hartlepool were tightly packed into the pews.

They discovered later that the minister, apparently overwhelmed by Nick's Irish ancestry, had recorded his father's first name as "Patrick" and not "Peter" on their marriage certificate. Lilian was

Wedding of Nick and Lilian.
Left to right: Martha, Davy, Nick, Lilian, Mary and Annie.

sure that this would cause problems for future generations who might want to trace their ancestry. It did.

Lil, who couldn't come to the wedding, had invited them to spend their honeymoon at Steeple Aston. Bill took them to Carlisle in time to catch the afternoon train to Oxford. During their week with Lil they spent a day in London. John, who had arranged to meet them in the capital, gave them a guided tour of all the sights. As Dick and Lil returned to Cumberland shortly afterwards, when they bought the Glebe farm near Hethersgill, Nick and Lilian always felt that they had been very fortunate to have this time together in Oxford.

Annie, meanwhile, had gone back to West Hartlepool with Bill and Andy and the boys to spend some time with them in their new house, 22 Hutton Avenue.

22 Hutton Avenue,
West Hartlepool.

The large, three-storied, semi-detached house, named Ingledene, was described in a 2004 conservation article as being the epitome of "Victorian Splendour." It was actually Edwardian, having been built in 1904. All the rooms were large and were heated by either coal or gas fires.

They could be cold in winter time. There were three attic bedrooms. One became a bedroom for the boys. The second became their playroom with a toy railway track as a permanent feature. The third was used as a box room.

Annie, who was able to enjoy a proper holiday for the first time in her life, stayed for a fortnight. They took her all around the area and she had plenty to talk about when she returned home.

It wasn't long before she learned that she was to have a third grandchild. Nick and Lilian told her that if the new baby, expected in June, 1939, was a boy he would be named Peter, after Nick's father. If it was a girl she would be named Anne. With the tragic loss of Kate's first baby indelibly printed in her memory, Lilian paid £5 to have a hospital delivery at Brampton Cottage Hospital and Annie went to High Bow Bank in time for the birth. The new grandchild arrived very quickly on Sunday 11th June. The sun was shining when Nick, returning from the 'phone box in Kirkhouse, walked into the house at High Bow Bank to give Annie the news.

"It's Anne," he said glumly, and sat down and stuck his nose in the newspaper.

Annie, not wanting to rub salt in the wound, ran into the scullery, punched the air with her fists, and jumped silently up and down for joy. As soon as Nick, who would not be allowed to visit the hospital until evening, had pulled himself together, begun to look happier, and gone off to give the news to everybody at High Fell, Annie burst into song and skipped around the kitchen table a few times before rushing out to tell the neighbours. So somebody was pleased.

The summer of 1939 was filled with apprehension. Hopes for peace were accompanied by preparations for war. On the 1st September the German army crossed the border into Poland. Two days later, for the second time in many people's lives, Britain was at war with Germany. Plans were made to evacuate the children from the cities to the safe haven of the countryside. In the early months of the 1914 war, German cruisers had shelled Hartlepool. Fearing an imminent repetition of this event, Bill and Andy arranged for six-year-old Robert and three-year-old Billy to be evacuated to Annie in Walton.

Minnie and Annie in the garden at Rose House.

Minnie, their maid, came as well, to help with all the work. So Annie, the former parlour maid, now found herself with a maid of her own. They soon built up a friendly relationship.

After a rather quiet year, Rose House was suddenly alive again with the voices of children. Annie, with her experience of the problems that could arise settling young children to sleep at night when they shared a room, decided that Robert should share her room. Billy shared the guest bedroom with Minnie. The arrangement worked well.

Life in Walton was very different to life in West Hartlepool. The boys' experiences of that time in their childhood would remain clearly etched in their adult memories. They remembered every detail of the design and furnishing of Rose House and of the village school just across the road. Going to bed by candlelight, and looking at the suffering face of the man who fell among thieves on the Good Samaritan picture, particularly impressed Robert. He could almost feel the pain. Visiting the outside lavatory in the dark was another trauma, which Annie eased by putting a small lamp, with a candle-like flame, on the landing windowsill. No German, she was sure, would spot it in the blackout. Upsets were more than balanced, however, by the joys of such things as watching the emptying of the scraps from the slop bucket in the back-kitchen onto the village green and seeing the geese, accompanied by various fowl, come running to clear everything up. The boys helped to look after the hens in the back yard. When one of the hens stopped laying Robert watched in amazement as Annie, asking the hen to mend its ways, ducked it encouragingly in the water butt. The hen duly resumed laying.

They remembered fetching the buckets of drinking water from the tap near the chapel and collecting the milk in jugs from Town Head Farm.

Apart from a few scary moments with the geese, Billy's favourite memory of Annie at this time was of her run-in with the billy-goat. The goat, tethered on the village green, had an aggressive temperament and soon picked out Billy as a likely victim. He charged at the small boy every time he walked past. Annie caught the goat head-on in one of his charges. She stood firmly in front of him, grabbed him by the horns, and shook him unmercifully, saying, "Oh you would, would you, you would would you...?"

The goat never bothered them again. Annie meted out similar treatment to an attacking gander, grabbing him by the neck and threatening to throttle him, but it was the belligerent goat's punishment that gave the most joy to the boys from the town.

They remembered fishing for tiddlers, with jam-jars and nets left over from the shop, in King Water, a shallow and relatively still part of the river, at the end of the village. Robert, one day, decided to carve a gun out of a piece of wood and, unknown to Annie, helped himself to the old shop bacon-knife from the drawer in the kitchen table. He almost removed his thumb and was left with a scar that ensured he never forgot the incident.

"She couldn't turn her back for five minutes," one of her nieces laughed when recalling Annie's evacuees.

Every Saturday they went into Brampton to collect their meat ration from the butcher and the yeast from the Co-op. Annie's meat coupons were with a butcher on the main street but another butcher, the one that she had helped with the setting-up of the Walton meat round, told her to send Robert into his shop every week to say, "Sausages for Mrs Irving, please." Her good deed had resulted in an extra supply of sausages for the duration of the war.

The privations of the war years, when one pack of sausages was a much appreciated extra, are beyond the imagination of later generations. People became expert at making do and mending and in producing nourishing meals from very few ingredients. The diets of young children were supplemented with government-provided orange juice and cod liver oil. The cod liver oil was definitely not appreciated by the recipients. As always in times of severe food shortage, it was those living in the towns who suffered the greatest deprivation. Farmers were not officially allowed to dispose of any of their produce privately. Everything had to be accounted for. Many became inventive in their efforts to help less fortunate members of their families.

Annie's sister Mary, living in Carlisle, was one of the many struggling to feed her family on meagre rations. Kate and Lil arranged to meet her every Saturday morning in the entrance to Binns' Department Store. As they stood chatting, Kate would push a parcel of eggs and a jointed rabbit into Mary's bag. At the same time, Mary's sons, Bill and Ray, would be opening the unlocked boot of Dick and Lil's car, in a pre-arranged spot, to remove the bags of vegetables and other produce that had been left for them.

Everybody strived to do their bit for the war effort. The radio kept them informed of the progress of the war. Nick and Davy, like other men in occupations that exempted them from joining the army, joined the Home Guard. It was all taken very seriously. As a fell runner, Nick was chosen to be a signaller for the Hallbankgate branch. He spent many nights and week-ends training on the fells. Convoys of army vehicles were to be seen regularly driving over the fell roads on training exercises.

Everyone was issued with gas masks. Children took their masks to school with them. There were special masks for babies that mothers were told to practice using so that their baby would not be alarmed if a real emergency should arise.

Annie, like other members of the Women's Institute, was recruited to make jam. The fruit was gathered locally and the sugar was provided by the government. Inspectors came regularly to Friarsgarth, where the Walton jam-making took place, to ensure that the highest standards were maintained. If the label was not perfectly straight on the jar, the jam would be rejected. School children and their families were recruited to gather rose-hips for syrup and sacks of nettles. Robert understood that the nettles, which were given to the Women's Institute for despatch, would be used for the production of medicines. Nettles were a gift to Britain from the Romans. Robert remembered the inhabitants of Rose House getting stung many times during their collection. He also remembered that whatever they did at Walton involved a lot of walking. Trudging up to the village from the lane end with Annie one day, they were about to be overtaken by a car.

"Look tired!" Annie instructed them. The motorist duly stopped and offered them all a lift.

Clothing growing families with the clothing coupons available required some ingenuity. Old and outgrown jumpers were unravelled so that the best of the wool could be re-used. Fair Isle patterns and multi-coloured stripes became very popular. New sleeves would be knitted for jumpers that had badly worn elbows. Annie's spare minutes were permanently occupied with the knitting of socks. Women took their knitting with them everywhere. Every social event and bus journey was accompanied by the clicking of needles. Lilian got many of her patterns from her "Womans Weekly" magazine which she swapped with Annie for the "Peoples Friend." The shortage of paper ensured that all publications were passed on and swapped many times. There were waiting lists for the Dandy and the Beano comics. Even after there was no one living at High Fell to enjoy these publications, they never cancelled their order, but brought the comics down to High Bow Bank.

Bill and Andy drove over to Walton as often as their petrol coupons and Bill's work allowed. They were expecting a new baby in May, 1940. A delighted Annie read out the news of the arrival of their sister, Jane, to Robert and Billy. They all waited eagerly for the baby to be brought over to see them.

The expected bombardment of Hartlepool didn't happen and the early panic about the boys' safety gradually subsided. By the spring of 1941, when Lilian was ordered complete bed-rest before the birth of her second baby, it was decided that it would be safe for the evacuees to return to Hartlepool. Annie went to keep house at High Bow Bank for a few months.

Annie with Bill and family on the village green.

When Nick returned from the 'phone box in Kirkhouse on St Patrick's day, he was smiling. "It's Peter," he said joyfully.

Annie grabbed Anne's hands and skipped her round on the spot. All she needed now was for this awful war to finish so that the generation that included her five grandchildren could grow up in peace. Apart from the times that she spent in Hartlepool, Annie visited High Bow Bank every week. Because the bus from Walton lane end didn't connect with the bus to Hallbankgate, she walked into Brampton every Thursday morning and caught the bus for the second half of her journey.

Anne and Peter,
1941.

Following the complications before and after Peter's birth, Lilian had several stays in hospital and Annie frequently had to pack her bag and come to the rescue. She would come walking cheerfully over the hill top at High Bow Bank, a bit like an older Mary Poppins. She would have a large bag in one hand, an umbrella in the other, and a beaming smile on her face. Whatever the emergency that sometimes awaited her – on one occasion Lilian had badly scalded her leg when lifting the kettle off the fire – she had to sit down immediately to play the ready-prepared snakes and ladders, ludo or snap – often before she had time to remove her hat and coat.

When left in charge of the housekeeping she was very careful not to waste a single penny. Nick, who was known never to complain about food, was heard to say to Lilian on one of her returns from hospital, "Please don't make any more bread pudding." Not many crumbs had been thrown away while Annie was holding the reins.

She was at High Bow Bank every year for Christmas and took charge of the plucking, cleaning and stuffing of the goose. The sage and onion stuffing was home made. Annie always got the goose for Hartlepool from her sister, Kate, now living at Cambeck Hill Farm near Walton lane end. She plucked and cleaned it ready for use and then parcelled it up and took it to Carlisle. It was transported to Hartlepool by the United Bus Company. There would always be a panic at the other end if it was a bit late in its arrival.

As country children, Anne and Peter accepted without question that Nick was going to wring the neck of the live goose that he had brought home, although they never witnessed the execution. He told them of how when he first went to High Fell he saw the farmer's wife come out into the yard with an axe and thought that she was going to chop some sticks. He watched as she grabbed a hen and, without further ado, chopped off its head. He then saw the headless chicken jump up and run around the yard. It had been quite sometime before he saw the funny side of that experience.

Christmas toys were scarce but Lilian made and dressed rag dolls. She also dressed a black china doll that Nick's sister had acquired in Brampton. Nick made a doll's house and cradle. He carved and painted a large sit-on engine out of an old tree trunk. He made wheel-barrows of various sizes. He also made a large sledge, that would seat five children, for the winter snow. Every year, wonderful parcels would arrive from Mary Irving in Blaydon, the only one of George Irving's family never to marry. Bikes, dolls prams and mechanical toys were usually second-hand.

When Italian prisoners of war were sent to work on the farms and some of them arrived at High Fell, Martha's heart went out to them and she invited them into her (already overcrowded) home. She desperately hoped that young men of the area, that she knew were prisoners of the Germans and Japanese, would also be kindly treated. The High Fell prisoners spent every evening around her fire-side and shared in family life. Some of them carved Christmas toys – like monkeys on sticks – for her grandchildren.

During the war years all the Irving family, including Annie, received regular food parcels from Australia. The descendants of

Abraham Graham (brother of Mary Ann), who had emigrated with William Irving in 1851, never lost touch with their roots. The label had come off one of the tins they had sent to Abe and Lizzie. The tin was the same size as others that had contained sponge puddings – so they boiled it. It was a tin of sugar.

11

SHINGLES IN THE SNOW

Germany surrendered in May 1945 and the 8th May was declared VE Day. There were parties and celebrations across the country. The new Labour Government was elected in July and the Welfare State was born. Food was still scarce and rationing continued but the first consignment of bananas reached Britain in February 1946. Later that year Annie's three younger grandchildren, Anne aged seven, Jane aged six, and Peter aged five, were among those who were able to taste their first banana.

The future was beginning to look brighter. Then came the terrible winter of 1947. The worst cold spell of the century descended on the country. The family at High Bow Bank woke up one Saturday morning to find the snow up to the bedroom windows. Fortunately, Nick always kept his large coal shovel indoors during the winter months. He climbed out of a bedroom window and cleared all the snow from the front of the house. The lonning was completely blocked. All the pipes were frozen. Nick pulled Anne and Peter on the sledge to collect buckets of water from a spring across the field.

Hallbankgate School was closed so they ran down the hedge tops of the lonning to meet Annie in Kirkhouse on her next visit and to take her back home with them over the fields. They thought that it was great fun to be living and playing in such a crisp, white, winter wonderland. It hadn't been much fun for the unfortunate tramp who, early one morning, had been found dead in the brickworks where he had apparently crawled for shelter.

The following Thursday Annie wasn't on the bus that stopped at Farlam lane end. Lilian was sure that there would be a letter next day. There wasn't. By Saturday they knew that something must be seriously wrong. Nick went into Brampton and hired a taxi to take him to Walton. At first there was no answer when he knocked on the door of Rose House. Neighbours quickly gathered to see what was amiss. They confessed that they hadn't seen Annie for a few days but had assumed that she was staying indoors because of the weather. Nick hammered on the door again and a forlorn face appeared at the bedroom window. She had been in bed with a raging temperature.

Dr Harry, from Brampton, was sent for and neighbours promised to look after the patient until Nick could return to take her to High Bow Bank. He had to find a gang of men to help him to dig out the lonning so that they could get a taxi up to the house. Word soon got around. Able bodied men from the area, including Davy from High Fell, suddenly appeared with their spades and shovels. Later that afternoon, Annie, desperately ill with shingles, was brought up the lonning to be nursed back to health.

There had been several deaths from 'flu' and many people expected Annie to join their numbers. Dr Harry visited regularly and her medicines had to be collected from a shelf in the dispensary at the surgery in Brampton. One of the bottles of medicine was particularly vile and Annie grimaced every time Lilian handed her a tablespoonful, as directed on the bottle. On his next visit Dr Harry spotted the evil tasting concoction on the bedroom mantelpiece.

"Ah," he said, "the missing stomach medicine."

The label on the bottle simply said, "Irving – Walton." It had been intended for Annie's neighbour, no relation, of the same name.

"Well," she said indignantly, "have I been taking old Ju's stomach medicine? Haven't I been bad enough without you all trying to poison me?" She was clearly on the mend.

Nick set her even more firmly on the road to recovery when he came home from work with the story of "Old Jack" in Kirkhouse, who had been one of the many struck down with 'flu'. He had not been expected to survive and was visited one night by his friend, the undertaker. Looking out of the window and seeing the swirling snow, the undertaker had said cheerfully, "If tha disn't mind Jack, Ah'll just measure thoo now and save mesen a journey the morrer."

Jack sprang up in bed and began to make a quick recovery. Once she had stopped laughing, Annie never looked back either.

She stayed at High Bow Bank until the spring and the fine weather arrived. Friends and relatives at Walton kept regular fires going at Rose House to make sure that it was fit for her return. Annie was grateful that none of them had lifted the lid on a large saucepan in her back kitchen. It contained some broth that she said was "growing whiskers" when she found it.

Recovering at High Bow Bank, 1947.

Nick and Lilian, who had always dreamed of owning their own house, decided to try and save even harder for a deposit. They wanted to have Annie to live with them permanently. In the past they had kept and bred canaries, rabbits and Rhode Island Red hens. They now decided to keep a pig – which they could do if they gave up their bacon ration – and to try their hands at poultry farming. In return for all the help that Nick gave him at harvest time, Eddie Telford, the Kirkhouse farmer, allowed him to fence off a corner of a field, build hen-houses, and invest in a hundred White Leghorns for free-range egg production. They were very much against the new battery-farming methods. Their venture was a great success.

A pig-sty and pen were built across the road from their house and Nick went to Carlisle market to buy his first piglet. He brought it home on the bus, held closely inside his jacket with only its snout peeping out. Anyone wanting to keep a pig had to be a member of a pig society so that they could have permission to purchase the pig-meal for the animal's food. Friends and family couldn't contain their hilarity when Nick became secretary of the Hallbankgate Pig Society.

Lilian loved their pig, named Nelson after the farmer from whom he was purchased. She was the one who fed him, tickled his back, and talked to him. She was distraught when the time came for him to fulfil his purpose, but bravely researched the making of sausages, black pudding and potted meat. Annie came for the pig-killing to help with all the work. Times had moved on, she said, from the pig-sticking of her childhood. Nick had engaged the Hallbankgate butcher to stun Nelson and make his demise as painless as possible. The tenants of the row of terraced cottages allowed the use of their combined wash house for the slaughter.

Lilian stayed in the house with Annie. Her obnoxious off-spring followed the pig, led meekly to his death by Nick and Davy, so that they could witness his killing. Fortunately, it was quick and seemingly painless, but they demanded that his bladder be given to them for a football, as Annie had described happening in her childhood. In later years they looked back in horror at how callously they had watched Nelson's end.

The war had speeded up the mechanisation of the pits. Davy and Nick, now travelling to work by motorbike, were making modest progress in their mining careers and were studying for their shot-firing and deputy-overman tickets. The conversations at home always seemed to be about conveyor belts and duck-bill loaders. The story was often told of the official who, on instructing new recruits in the use of one piece of machinery, had firmly told them, "Never stick your finger in this hole." To make sure that they understood the hole to which he was referring, he helpfully stuck in his own finger. It was duly chopped off.

Annie liked the story of the pit rat and never tired of listening to Davy's account. Rats were part of the pit environment and were always chewing through the men's bait bags, which held their tins of sandwiches, to try and get at the food. They would gather hungrily around when the food was being consumed. Pit props were kept at hand for beating them off. One man, who had put on his jacket for warmth while he was eating, suddenly felt a rat run up his back. He closed the jacket tightly around himself, trapping the rat. Turning his back to a friend he said, "Quick. Belt it with that prop." The friend obligingly grabbed the prop and, in spite of Davy telling him to stop, whacked it against the man's back. He killed the rat – and put the owner of the jacket out of action for the rest of the shift.

In West Hartlepool, following the birth of the National Health Service, Bill decided to give up General Practice. He took his F.R.C.S.Ed. in 1946 and, to Annie's delight, was appointed Consultant Surgeon to the Hartlepool Group of Hospitals in 1948. She always found it amusing that he was no longer Dr Irving, but Mr. Irving. Bill became widely known and highly respected for his pioneering work. The Northern Daily Mail later quoted a colleague who wrote that Bill "was probably the most respected member of his profession that we had in the Hartlepools. As a surgeon he was without equal. He was a man who never dilly-dallied but got on with the job, and consequently he dealt with three or four times as many surgical cases as anyone else. His work was beyond praise. He never fussed or worried or lost his temper with his staff. Everyone who came into contact with him just loved him."

He was an energetic member of the B.M.A. — eventually becoming president of the Tees-side Branch. He was a member of the North of England Surgical Society and of the Newcastle and Northern Counties Medical Society. He was also a Fellow of the Association of Surgeons of Great Britain and Ireland.

Bill and Andy decided to invest in private education for their family. When Annie heard that thirteen-year-old Robert was to go as a boarder to Epsom College in Surrey in 1946, she was devastated. She knew all about the horrors of boarding schools, she told them. She had read Dickens, the Brontes and, worst of all, Tom Brown's School Days. Although she was convinced that it was nothing other than child cruelty, this was one battle she didn't win. She cried as she sewed on Robert's name tapes, imagining all the terrors that awaited him. It was probably just as well that nobody communicated her feelings to Robert. His first letter was so cheerful and funny that she began to feel a bit better, but she carried all his letters in her bag and scrutinised them minutely for signs of hidden suffering.

At High Bow Bank, in the spring of 1948, Anne, off school as she was frequently, with bronchitis, was suddenly struck by a terrible pain in her side. Lilian thought that it must be appendicitis. Nick came home from work to find Dr Harry in attendance and Lilian in a state of collapse.

"It's bronchial pneumonia," Dr Harry told him. "We'll have to get her into the Cottage Hospital. There's a new drug I can treat her with."

"I can't take her," said Lilian desperately, remembering the deaths of so many of her young cousins.

Nick wrapped Anne in a blanket and took her by taxi to the hospital before going on to Walton to get Annie to come to Lilian. A few days later, Anne awoke in the Cottage Hospital, now the memorial for the fallen soldiers of two wars, to see two faces beaming at her. Annie and Martha had come together to see for themselves the miracle of the new wonder drug, penicillin.

The search for a new house that would suit both Annie and the family at High Bow Bank was now well under way. Annie was suffering badly with aches and pains in her joints, later diagnosed as rheumatoid arthritis, that were not helped by her living conditions. She suffered agonies with cramp in her legs during the night. Although electricity was now available to all in the village, she refused to have it installed at Rose House. She had visited neighbours' houses that had been connected and was adamant that she wasn't going to have her wallpaper ruined by all those dangerous wires running all over the place. She was, she said, perfectly alright with her oil-lamps and candles. She agreed to move if Nick and Lilian found a suitable place for them all, but she was happy in Walton, where she had her own routine and circle of friends. She went to church every Sunday morning and chapel every Sunday evening, when she provided supper for the visiting local preacher.

Rose House remained a wonderful place, full of surprises, for her grandchildren to come and stay. Annie remembered being wakened in the large feather bed one moonlit night by an eerie creaking sound on the road outside.

"It's only Jane Watson cleaning up," said Annie.

Jane Watson lived in "The Green" cottage in front of Rose House. Like her mother before her, Jane had been "taken advantage of" as a young woman. Jane's son, now grown up, lived and worked on a farm away from the village. In earlier years he had lived in the two-roomed cottage with his mother and grandmother. Jane, born in 1895, followed the pattern of housekeeping established by her mother and cleaned up the tiny cottage only when the ashes from the grate reached the door and the empty food tins on the table completely covered the surface. She then waited till the rest of the village were in bed and spent the night barrowing the rubbish to the ash-tip. Unfortunately, the wheel of her barrow was never oiled.

Jane never washed either her clothes or herself and, although Annie didn't turn her away when she came visiting, she was always kept near the open door so that the worst of the smells could be wafted out with her when she left. When Jane's mother had died, some years ago, it was Annie who, during the night, had been called to attend the death and make sure that a doctor was in attendance.

"Are you sure you can cope, Mrs Irving?" the doctor had asked sympathetically before leaving her to sort everything out.

Annie had made Jane clean up the living room while she herself had cleaned up the bedroom.

"It was a yard brush and wheelbarrow job before I could take my scrubbing brushes and 'Jeyes fluid' round," said Annie. She carried the buckets of hot water round from Rose House. She

ANNIE O' THE MILL

then washed and laid out the body in one of her own
nightdresses. She also provided the linen for the bed. She worked
all night and had everything respectable before the rest of the
village was about. She even managed to persuade Jane to have a
wash. Jane had cried and said that she had never seen her mother
look so beautiful. After the funeral she reverted to her old ways.

Jane delivered the post for Walton and the surrounding area for
many years. Although she was provided with a bike, she never
actually learned to ride and pushed it around on her daily
marathon. One day, the men from the Mill saw her walking past
one of the fields while they were working and one of them
called, "Cock your leg over the saddle, Jane. It'll be a lot faster."

"Giv' ovva," was Jane's reply. "Ah's in a hurry."

Jane eventually ended her days happily in an old people's home
in Carlisle where she was kept clean, warm and comfortable.
When she was brought back to Walton for burial only the family
from Walton Mill remembered her.

It was during Annie's last year at Rose House, in 1949, that she
was cold-called by an insurance man anxious for her to take out
a policy. She politely declined but, to her annoyance, he
persisted. Then he made his big mistake.

"It's your duty to your children," he told her, "to make sure that
they are not left with any bills when you die."

"Duty to my children!" Annie exclaimed furiously. "Don't you
dare talk to me about my duty to my children. I've spent my life
doing my duty."

As she had done with the governess so long ago, she grabbed her
sweeping brush and set about the ankles of the unfortunate

insurance salesman.

"Get off with you," she shouted as she swept him out. "If there isn't any money to bury me with, they'll just have to leave me to rot."

As he ran down the path, she called after him, "When the stink gets bad enough somebody will dig a hole and chuck me in."

The man left the village at speed. He seemed to have lost the will to make any more cold calls that day.

Nick and Lilian were outbid at auctions several times before, in 1950, they bought 6 Ridgevale Terrace on Lanercost Road in Brampton by private treaty. It cost £2,000. Annie was thrilled. Her friend Mrs Bawden had lived at Ridgevale Terrace and she could see the shelter on the Sands, with the millstone from Walton Mill on top, from the front bedroom window.

Annie had a massive sort out, and several bonfires, before she left Rose House. Her giant wedding picture and most of her Victorian texts and pictures were among the casualties – but The Good Samaritan was saved for posterity to take pride of place above her bed in the new house. She followed the family's instructions and threw away any clothes that were no longer fit for wear, except for a pair of old whale-bone corsets. Lilian said afterwards that she couldn't think of an occasion when Annie had imagined they might be useful. Annie hid them right at the bottom of her massive bedding chest. Unfortunately, the chest was so heavy that the removal men unpacked it. The old whale-bone corsets were wonderfully draped over a pile of blankets that were carried into the new house in full view of all interested neighbours.

Davy had helped Nick to remove the bedroom window to get the wardrobe out the day before they left High Bow Bank. The

removal men came there first before going on to Walton for
Annie. It didn't take long to load their possessions. Nick had
bought a car two years earlier, but they could never persuade
Bob, their much-loved border collie, to get into it. Once, when
someone had left the field gate open, Bob had proudly brought a
sheep into the kitchen. On the day of the removal he was the
first one into the car.

They took one last look at the old house as they went over the
hilltop to start their new life, but the memories would remain.
The sight of the violets by the beck, the banks of primroses and
cowslips, and the delicate, often solitary, harebells; the smell of
new mown hay; the scrunch of autumn leaves, the bleating of the
spring lambs, the songs of the dawn chorus and the comforting
sound of the wind through the beech trees; the joy of the
dandelion clocks, the daisy chains, the butter cups, the bluebells,
the conkers and the brambles; the soothing relief of dock leaves
after nettle stings; and the wonderful whiteness of the silent winter
snow, never dirtied by traffic, would belong to them for life.

The new house was one of seven in an attractive terrace. It had a
vestibule, hall, two large reception rooms, a pantry, and a
kitchen with a gas cooker and room for Lilian's Hotpoint washing
machine. A back boiler in the living room provided a constant
supply of hot water. The bathroom was on the first floor where
Annie, Anne and Peter each had a bedroom. Annie had the
largest front bedroom. The front sitting room was also designated
for her use, although she preferred to spend her time in the
kitchen. Nick and Lilian had the front attic bedroom. Amazingly,
when the electricity supply was installed it hadn't been thought
necessary to extend it to the attics. So Lilian was back to candles
and torches. They also had Annie's beautiful brass bedstead, now
considered very old fashioned, in their attic bedroom. Probably

worth a small fortune today, the bedstead was taken to the tip in 1954. Another act of vandalism, by today's standards, was carried out in Annie's front sitting room when the original Victorian fireplace was taken out to make room for a modern tiled grate. A new Wilton carpet and brown leather three-piece suite were also bought for her sitting room. Over the next few months, Lilian re-papered all the rooms. She had made a complete set of new curtains before they took up residence.

Nick, Lilian and Peter in the backyard at Ridgevale Terrace.

As each member of her extended family came to visit and see the house, Annie took them straight into the kitchen to admire the sink, the two taps and the constant supply of hot water. No one else was allowed to touch the washing-up. That was her privilege. She regularly went round inspecting cupboards for crockery that she felt was in dire need of her attention. She was, she said, in heaven at that sink.

Her three sisters, Mary, Lil and Kate, were the most frequent family visitors and the conversations when they all got together in the sitting room were incredible. Anne would usually be curled up in a chair, doing what she did best, reading a book. The more interesting the conversations became, the less frequently were the pages of the book turned.

"This is better than any book," she thought to herself.

Anne, and later Peter, was among those who benefited from the advent of the Grammar Schools. The old Secondary School in

Brampton became the White House Grammar School. Along with her friend from birth, Jean Mitchell, Anne delighted Annie by passing her eleven plus just before they left High Bow Bank, and shortly before the outbreak of the Korean War. She was one of the two-form-entry of 1950. Perhaps it was the environment. Of the seven children who lived at Bow Bank during the war years, five went to the Grammar School.

As well as her wheezy chest, Anne was afflicted with poor eyesight. They had been on a family visit to Mary in Carlisle when Anne, aged three, began to rub her suddenly inflamed left eye. Mary took them all straight round to the infirmary where they were told that her prompt action had probably saved the little sight that was left in the eye. It was another fifty years before an optometrist explained that, in cases like this, the brain does not equalise the sight from both eyes. It simply switches off the bad eye, making hand/eye co-ordination difficult, as well as limiting the field of vision. All sorts of minor problems, such as inability to hit a rounders ball, judging the level of liquid when pouring a cup of tea, and walking past friends in a busy street without seeing them, were suddenly explained.

Soon after their arrival in Brampton Nick was cleaning the car in the lay-by across the road with Bob beside him. Anne came out of the house and called the dog over to her. She hadn't seen the motorbike coming down the road to her left. The rider was unhurt, but Bob was killed, shockingly and outright in front of her.

12

WHAT KEPT YOU?

Nick alternated between day shift and afternoon shift at work and now travelled by bus from the end of Tree Road on the other side of the Sands. When he was on afternoons it was usually eleven o'clock at night before he rang the front door bell when he got home. Lilian worried a lot about his safety at work and the possibility of a terrible pit accident. One winter's night the door bell was rung a little earlier than Nick's expected time. Lilian opened the door to find a policeman on the step. She didn't seem able to comprehend his words when he asked, officiously, "Have you got a dog licence, madam?"

Annie came to the rescue. "Are you Sergeant Brown?" she asked. She had read about Sergeant Brown in the Cumberland News.

The policeman drew himself up to his full height and puffed out his chest. "No, madam. I'm P.C. Eccleston."

"I thought you wouldn't be Sergeant Brown," said Annie. "He'd have more sense than to come frightening the life out of folk at this time of night, just to see if they had a dog licence when they haven't even got a dog. Be off with you."

One black night shortly afterwards Nick was walking back across the Sands when he heard footsteps stalking him. Thinking he was about to be mugged, the one-time fell-runner increased his speed, eventually breaking into a sprint. The mugger followed, puffing and panting, and gradually losing ground, behind him. Nick ran up the path to the house and rang the bell before turning with his bag clutched in his hand ready, he said later, to fell the villain with his bait tin. Lilian opened the door to see a policeman grabbing Nick with the words, "Got you! Going to rob these poor folk were you?"

"He lives here," said Lilian indignantly. "He's just come home from work."

By this time Annie was on the scene. She wouldn't be silenced.

"I know you," she said, "you're that P.C. Eccleston. I don't know what Sergeant Brown's thinking about letting the likes of you prowl around at night tormenting innocent folk. You're just like those stupid policemen that accused my Rob of burglary in Newcastle. He was out half the night. I didn't know what had kept him."

The constable made a hasty retreat. He didn't bother them again. Annie spent a lot of time these days remembering times long gone and people like Abe and Lizzie, who had both died in 1949, and who had played such a big part in her life. She took advantage of her easy access to bus and car transport to visit many old friends and places. Petrol rationing had ended in 1950. Her first visit was to George and Ray in Blaydon. Annie took Anne along with her on many bus trips to surrounding towns and villages and on a week's visit to "Preston Annie" – the bother with Bonzo long since forgotten. While they were at Preston they heard the announcement on the wireless that Princess Elizabeth was to name her new daughter Anne. All three of them admired her choice.

Annie also spent a lot of time at Hartlepool where, true to form, she stationed herself in the kitchen whenever they were entertaining. Their helper, Mrs Robinson, was, she said, much easier to talk to than all those hospital people. Mrs Robinson, who came daily, had replaced their last live-in helper who had been associated with an intruder trying to steal Andy's jewellery.

Andy had walked into their bedroom and seen a pair of feet sticking out from under the bed. She was reported in the paper as saying, "Will the owner of the feet come out from under the bed?"

The intruder rushed past her, wrestled with Bill on the stairs, and escaped. Although later arrested he escaped retribution on a technicality. The police charged him with "breaking and entering" which was not strictly the case. Bill converted the attic room vacated by the maid into a workshop for his woodworking hobby. The carpenter's son produced many fine pieces of furniture and intricate carvings in this room.

"Rob would have been proud of him," Annie said.

Billy had now followed Robert, who would soon be going to University, to school in Epsom. Jane would go to Harrogate. Annie was especially proud of Jane's musical talent.

"I've got five very different grandchildren," she told her sisters. "I won't be here to see what they make of their lives, but I hope they'll be happy in whatever they choose to do, and I hope they'll remember me kindly."

There was one particular place that Annie wanted to revisit – Morley Street, in Newcastle. The family from Ridgevale Terrace all went with her on this pilgrimage, which was combined with a visit to George and Sally in Felling. She sat in the car outside her old home for a few minutes and then asked to go back to Brampton by the route that she had followed with the horse and dray in 1911. She never mentioned it again.

National events concentrated her thoughts on the future and progress into a "New Age," most of which, having passed her three-score-years-and-ten, she knew she would miss. George V1 died suddenly in February 1952, the month that Churchill announced Britain's development of an atomic bomb. Anne's class were in a music lesson when the caretaker walked purposefully into the room and, in a loud stage whisper, told Mr. S.A.G. Macey (known as Sag), "The king's dead." Sag regularly enthused his pupils by telling them how glad he was that he was not of their generation, which was destined to witness Armageddon with all the wickedness that surrounded them, and the nuclear war that would surely finish them off. On receiving the news of the king's death, he treated them all to some funeral dirges played slowly on the piano.

The king was genuinely mourned by the people and there was great sympathy for the new young queen who had to be hastily flown home from Kenya. Annie wondered if she would reign for as long as Victoria, and hoped that the catalogue of disasters that saw out 1952 would be replaced by happier things. There were terrible floods in Lynmouth, air and rail disasters, and a London smog that killed four thousand people in four days.

Annie was particularly devastated, in 1952, by the trouble that hit Walton Mill. Edna had been married to Irving, who helped Bob and Tom to farm both the Mill and the adjoining Hillhead farm, for some years. The young couple lived at Hillhead. They had three children. On the 15th September the men from the farm had been moving the cows from one of the Mill fields. Irving stayed in the field to collect the bull – normally a placid animal. The bull turned on him and gored him twice. Irving slid himself to the edge of the field shouting for help. The bull, whose vision was restricted by a tin shield on his face, lost him for a short time but went round the side of the field and came up to him again by the dyke. Irving managed to hold onto the bull's ring until help arrived.

The bull had smashed his pelvis, hip and femur. Edna arrived at the Mill from Hillhead to find an ambulance, Dr. Harry, and her mother, Edie, ready to go to the Infirmary with them. The bone that was originally used on the grafts was too soft and gave way. Irving lay in a hospital bed from September to May with his leg held up. Altogether he was in hospital for a year and ten days. Mary, and her house in Carlisle, became a refuge for Edna during the stress of Irving's suffering and hospitalisation. He never fully recovered his previous good health. They eventually left Hillhead and went to live in Walnut Cottage in Walton where Edna ran the village post office for many years.

The proposed culling of the rabbit population was another major concern of 1952. By then, the rabbits, that had saved so many from starvation in times of crisis, had become a major threat to crop production. The problem had been solved in Australia by the use of the cruel myxomatosis virus. Europe decided to follow suit. Two wild rabbits were inoculated with the disease in northern France. Nothing else was needed. The disease was spread widely by numbers of mosquitoes, fleas, ticks, mites and lice, as well as by actual contact between individual rabbits. Infection spread rapidly over vast areas. By 1953, the English countryside was blighted by the sight of vast numbers of suffering rabbits and hares.

Davy, who walked daily on the fells, was continually distressed by the appalling spectacle of rabbits sitting motionless on the grass with swollen heads and inflamed, oozing eyes. Those that

Davy on his beloved fells.

were not put out of their misery

by compassionate passers-by took two weeks to die. The rabbit population was decimated, but some survived, built up an immunity and began to re-populate. Annie, who saw some of the suffering in the field across the road from Ridgevale Terrace, wondered what the world was coming to. If this was scientific progress and modern life in England, she wanted none of it. The country lost its appetite for rabbit pies and stews.

The coronation, planned for June 1953, concentrated minds on happier hopes for the future and was a much needed opportunity for national rejoicing. Spirits were further raised by the launching of the Royal Yacht in April, by the conquering of Everest in May, and by the promised end of the Korean War. There were coronation parties and celebrations locally and nationally. Lilian planted the border of their small front garden with red geraniums, white alyssum and blue lobelia. The grammar school pupils, conducted by Sag, sang *Land of Hope and Glory* on the school field. Beacons were lit countrywide.

They didn't have a television but Annie listened to coverage on the wireless and avidly read the newspaper accounts. When she heard that a film of her "last coronation" was to be shown in colour at the Botchergate Cinema in Carlisle she was determined to see it. With Lilian, Anne and Peter, she travelled to Carlisle and joined the long queue snaking down Botchergate for the continuous showing. Her legs were now in a terrible state with her arthritis but she gritted her teeth and stood – a supreme example of mind over matter and sheer determination. Several times Lilian suggested going home. They were finally allowed in for the third showing since they had joined the queue. Annie said it was worth it. The other three weren't so sure. After another long wait at the bus stop in Warwick Road, the Newcastle bus dropped them off at the Sands.

"I've watched that go round a good few times," Annie said once again as they trudged past the millstone on the shelter.

Annie and Anne at Ridgevale Terrace, 1953.

Annie spent many of the hot summer days of 1953 sitting on a specially bought canvas chair just outside the front door. She watched the world go by, admired the brightly coloured flowers in the garden, and dipped into the Cumberland News and the Peoples Friend. She was also very interested in the content of the recently introduced Eagle and Girl comics.

In October she found a lump in her abdomen. She went into the Infirmary at about the time Irving was coming out. There were several distressing and painful investigations and a particularly unpleasant nursing sister in charge of the ward.

On one of her visits, Mary was convinced that not enough was being done to relieve her sister's pain. Bill was in regular communication with the consultant in charge of her case. One morning the ward sister was thrown into a state of agitation by a sudden visit to Annie from a posse of doctors led by the consultant and Bill.

"Are they looking after you?" Bill asked.

Annie saw the sister flush as she looked straight at her.

"Yes," she said quietly, "everybody is very kind."

She was upset after that to find that she suddenly mattered. The sister couldn't do enough for her. Her pain was noted and drugs were prescribed. Annie fumed to Lilian, "Whether I'm a consultant's mother or a miner's mother-in-law shouldn't matter. But it does in this ward – and I don't like it. I thought this National Health Service was supposed to be the same for everybody."

It was while she was in hospital that the shattering and life-changing news was broken to the miners that the fell pits were shortly to close, forcing either redundancies on a large scale, or relocation – then a major upheaval – within six months to another part of the country. Annie had just been diagnosed with terminal bowel cancer. Their world, as they knew it, was coming to an end.

"We won't tell her about the pits," Lilian decided.

On their next visit Annie was sitting up in bed waiting for them. She passed Lilian a newspaper with the story of the pit closures prominently displayed. The expression on her face said everything.

"The papers always make things look worse than they are," Lilian told her. "It's going to take time to wind things down and there'll be jobs for quite a while yet." Lilian always tried to be optimistic in the face of impending disaster.

The sister came to see them at the bedside.

"Now dear," she said to Lilian, "we've explained to your mother that she can be discharged from hospital now, but she's going to need a lot of looking after. If you like we can arrange for her to go into a nursing home."

Annie looked at Lilian. "She's coming home." Lilian said firmly.

A fire was lit in the front bedroom ready for the patient's

return. It was kept going day and night for almost two months. The coal had to be carried upstairs in buckets. Nick's coal allowance was extremely useful. A commode was installed beside the bed and a comfortable armchair placed beside the fire. Annie needed round-the-clock nursing. The drugs that controlled the pain also caused terrifying hallucinations. Lilian was running up and downstairs from the attic at night, and up and downstairs from the kitchen in the daytime. There was a steady stream of visitors to be entertained. After the end of the first week, Annie's three sisters arrived together.

"We've decided," they told Lilian, "we're going to take it in turns to come and stay at night to do the night shifts." They did just that until the next weekend when Bill and Andy came to visit.

"They won't be able to keep this up," Bill said. "It's going to get a lot harder. If we can find a local nurse to come and sit with her every night, I'll meet the cost."

Nick went to see Nurse Betty Forrest, the retired district nurse from Hallbankgate, who now lived in School Lane in Brampton. She started that night. She also arranged for her sister-in-law, Margaret, to come and help Lilian with the housework in the daytime. Bill met this cost as well. Nurse Forrest became a firm friend to all of them as she quietly took charge of the sick room. Annie got progressively worse and was not expected to be with them for Christmas. Although she understood everything that was going on around her, she lost the ability to speak. One morning Lilian found her agitated and trying to communicate something. She kept looking hard at Lilian and the nurse, and then at the drawer at the bottom of her wardrobe.

She nodded when Lilian asked, "Do you want us to get something out of that drawer?"

Hidden in a corner of the drawer, among all her "laying-out" clothes, was a wad of money.

Annie nodded again when Lilian asked, "Do you want me to look after this for you?"

The insurance man needn't have worried. She wasn't going to leave her family with any funeral bills to settle. When Bill and Andy visited them on the Saturday, almost a week before Christmas day, Annie was drifting in and out of consciousness. Bill said that it would only be a matter of days. Lilian suddenly had another worry.

"All the shops will be shut over Christmas," she said. "What on earth am I going to do? I've only got a cream coloured coat. I'll shame her at her funeral."

"No you won't," said Andy practically. "You all go into Carlisle now and get whatever you need. We'll hold the fort here."

Lilian was aghast. She'd never heard of anybody doing such a thing as buying funeral clothes before the death. Bill persuaded her.

"You know she'd be tickled pink at the thought," he said. "And you know that she'd far rather you did that than go to her funeral in a cream coat!"

So they went to Carlisle. The assistant in the shop was extremely helpful and obviously deeply sympathetic that someone had suffered a bereavement just before Christmas. As she was wrapping up the purchases, she asked, "When's the funeral, dear?"

Lilian made a choking sound and seemed unable to speak. Anne ran outside to wait for them on the pavement. Nobody spoke on the way home. On the Monday, Annie slipped into a deep, peaceful coma. Nurse Forrest said that they would probably lose her in the night, but if she survived it would be the next night.

"Two o'clock in the morning is always the low time," she said. "It always happens then. You can still talk to her while she's like this. The hearing is always the last thing to go."

Annie was still there, four days later, on Christmas morning. They all quietly wished her a "Happy Christmas." They turned up the volume on the wireless so that she could hear the Christmas carols.

The words of her favourite carol had never seemed so poignant.

> *"And our eyes at last shall see Him,*
> *Through His own redeeming love;*
> *For that child so dear and gentle*
> *Is our Lord in heaven above;*
> *And He leads his children on*
> *To the place where He is gone.*
>
> *Not in that poor lowly stable,*
> *With the oxen standing by*
> *We shall see Him, but in Heaven*
> *Set at God's right hand on high,*
> *Where like stars, His children crowned*
> *All in white shall wait around."*

As they pushed their Christmas dinner around their plates, Lilian said that it was worse than the Christmas thirty years ago when her Aunt Maggie had dropped down dead at Heads Nook, on Christmas Eve, while she was making her mince pies. Hysteria threatened. As always, comedy and tragedy wrestled for supremacy.

"They sent the telegrams on Christmas Eve," Lilian continued, "and her parcels of Christmas presents arrived on Christmas Day."

Annie finally left them, to live their lives without her, in the early hours of Boxing Day. At the end of her tunnel of light, Rob would surely be waiting, with his familiar grin, and a well remembered, "What kept you?"

End